PTSD: Frozen in Time

Adventures in Releasing Buried Energy

Ann E. Laurie

PTSD: FROZEN IN TIME
Adventures in Releasing Buried Energy
Copyright © 2015 by Ann E. Laurie. All rights reserved.

For JFS

"We shall not cease from exploration
And the end of all our exploring
Will be to arrive where we started
And know the place for the first time."

—T.S. Eliot, "Little Gidding"

Contents

Preface 1

General Outline of My Life (As It Relates to PTSD)....................3

Shake, Rattle and Roll: Releasing Buried Energy............................8

The Big Hurt: The Physical Pain of Buried Emotion 13

As Tears Go By: Releasing Stress Hormones 17

Hello, It's Me: Mindful Meditation of the Body 20

Strange Things Happen in This World: Frozen Time
    and Parallel Universes..24

Let's Go Get Stoned: Painkillers and PTSD..............................29

Lush Life: Why People With PTSD Get Monster Hangovers .... .33

Help! How Your Body Reacts to Terror.......................................36

Crazy: When You Feel Like Killing Someone Because There Is
    Fruit Residue on the Underside of Your Kitchen Cabinet
    Knobs..38

Feelings: My Key Code for Somatic Pain 41

Bless the Beasts and the Children: My Visit to the Shaman..........46

It's Only a Paper Moon: *The Matrix* and the PTSD Brain 53

Is That All There Is? My Experience with Craniosacral Therapy ..57

Kind of a Drag: The Demoralization of Dissociation 59

Knock Three Times (or Five or Seven): The Tapping Solution
    (Emotional Freedom Technique)..61

Sorry Seems to Be the Hardest Word: Does an Apology
    Make Any Difference? 64

Who Can I Turn To: My Visit to the Energy Healer 67

Music, Music, Music 72

Splish, Splash: How to Clean Your Aura 75

What's Going On? Trauma Releasing Exercises 78

Oh, Happy Day: The Chiropractor... 83

Hello, Goodbye: Leaving the Freeze State 86

Smile: PTSD Teeth.. 89

Imagine: Intrusive Thoughts 91

Both Sides Now: Another Look at Nausea 94

Do It Again: Somatic Therapy 96

Tell Me Why: Did I Choose to Have PTSD for
    This Incarnation?... 100

Cry Me a River: Trauma Releasing Exercises (TRE)
    —One Year Later 104

Spooky: Residual Hauntings and Trauma Energy 107

You Are Not Alone: The Secret Life of Plants 109

Hurts So Bad: When Stomach Pain Wakes You in the Night.... 112

Gonna Take a Miracle: All the Pain I Never Felt....................... 116

Epilogue.. 122

Postscript 124

Recommended Reading (In alphabetical order)......................... 125

About the Author.. 131

Other Titles by Ann E. Laurie.. 132

To Wee or Not to Wee (Guest Essay by Lori A. O'Connell) 135

Startle: A True Story of PTSD and the Paranormal................... 141

Ghost Smeller: Adventures of a Low-Status Medium 157

Preface

For over twenty years, my PTSD symptoms were sufficiently controlled by medication such that I could sleep at night, keep a job, and live a relatively pain-free life. It was also a life of isolation, alienation, dissociation, hypervigilance and despair, but you can't have everything.

I was in talk-therapy with psychiatrists during this period, too.

In my late-forties, the meds slowly but surely stopped working, and every symptom I experienced in my twenties eventually returned: insomnia, severe physical pain without organic cause, sense of a foreshortened future, startle effect, night terrors, intrusive thoughts, feelings of depersonalization and derealization, unpredictable cycling between hyperarousal and dissociation, emotional numbness and despair. All those fifty-minute hours of talking, talking, talking and all those prescribed medications had apparently healed nothing. The trauma energy that flooded me in childhood, when I could neither fight nor flee, remained inside me.

Pills and talk therapy were no longer my solutions. Numbing my feelings with chemicals and talking about traumatic events pretty much shut down my survival brain all those years when it was my survival brain which needed engaging. But how was I to communicate with it when it only spoke and interpreted reality through the senses, and had no means of understanding language? This was going to be a challenge.

I was prepared to try just about anything to release that buried energy since it came to manifest in physical pain so severe, it

1

sometimes left me gasping for breath or curled up in a fetal position, sobbing. I had to take action, and inexpensive action at that, since I'd been on a limited budget after losing my job in the recession of 2008.

I've written here of my adventures over the last three years in pursuit of healing my PTSD with non-traditional methods, as well as general thoughts on related issues. I do not detail the nature of my original trauma, which occurred over a four-year period in my childhood. Talking about what happened long ago proved, over the years, to do little more than nail those memories deeper and deeper into my psyche without the benefit of any relief. Other times I retraumatized myself by telling the stories again. I also find words inadequate to convey the anguish, terror and violence to the soul suffered under trauma. Suffice it to say that when I was safe again, the trauma energy was not discharged and I developed the symptoms of PTSD, although I would not know for many years what was wrong with me.

These essays, originally published on a short-lived blog, can be read independently, although they might make more sense if read from the beginning when I describe chronologically what happened after I got off medication. Because these essays were written as stand-alone narratives online, there may be repetition among them although I've edited to reduce their occurrence.

I also include at the end of the essays, two short-reads I published separately having to do with PTSD and the paranormal.

Thank you for taking a look at my book, Dear Reader. I found PTSD to be a lonely condition and have felt less alone writing these essays, imagining one day that you might read them—and understand.

December, 2015

General Outline of My Life
(As It Relates to PTSD)

If you are outline-averse, feel free to skip this section. The basics, fleshed out below, are the following: I was in a state of fight-or-flight for four years as a child, during and after which, I did not discharge the vast energy mobilized within to deal with the perceived threat. I spent the next thirty to forty years unknowingly blocking the release of the original trauma energy, first with alcohol, then drugs—both doctor prescribed and self-prescribed.

Then one day, the meds stopped working.

You can skip to the first essay now if you like.

1965-1970
Age nine to thirteen. I could not fight or flee during this period of trauma, so I froze. The vast energy mobilized to deal with the perceived threat unpredictably cycled between states of hyperarousal and dissociation with no outlet.

1970-1974
High school. I began drinking regularly by sophomore year. I did not understand why I felt what I felt (unpredictable emotional and physical numbness, dissociation, insomnia, hypervigilance, hyperarousal, anger inappropriate to context, sense of foreshortened future, startle effect, intrusive thoughts, reduced ability to concentrate, feeling unreal, despair), but drinking sure seemed to fix it—for a little while at least.

1974-1978
College. My drinking quickly grew out of control with black-outs and Jekyll/Hyde behavior. I quit drinking sophomore year and shortly thereafter became addicted to tranquilizers. My tolerance grew quickly and I ended up having to withdraw cold turkey when my supply dried up. (Living hell!) I began avoiding all social contact, only showing up to class to turn in papers and take exams. I felt physically and emotionally numb, which developed into despair at feeling so dead while all around me kids my age seemed to be having the time of their lives. I felt depressed, alienated and ashamed. I also began to feel inherently offensive, as if my mere physical presence in the proximity of others could somehow harm them. I felt this way on and off for about the next fifteen years.

1978-1979
I left school to take care of my mother who was dying of cancer. My PTSD symptoms intensified. My mother died at the end of '79.

1980
I felt no organic desire to do anything at all. For lack of a better idea, I went back to college.

1981-1982
I quit college, began drinking again and worked a series of short-term jobs.

1982-1985
I quit drinking for good and joined an addiction support group. The longer I was sober, the more PTSD symptoms emerged, plus new ones like near-constant fatigue and baffling, debilitating physical pain everywhere in my body.

1986-1991

I stopped attending my addiction support group meetings due to my discomfort at feeling so much anger. I simply couldn't bear to be around anyone and went back to avoiding unnecessary social interaction. A psychiatrist diagnosed me with PTSD and prescribed Imipramine (and many more drugs over the years from Abilify to Zyprexa.) I quit working in bookstores due to the low pay and took a series of office jobs.

1991-1995

I blacked out on new tranquilizing meds for five days. My behavior was irrational and bizarre. I was committed to a psychiatric ward where I was re-diagnosed with PTSD. Losing my freedom snapped me out of my despair. After I was released, I made a tremendous effort to avoid all negative thoughts. I felt better and began a new well-paying career. I dated a lot of interesting men, but never got too close. Flashbacks began and ended in this period, never to return.

1995 - 2001

Although my career soared, I was in despair or numb most of these years. I continued trying new drugs my psychiatrist prescribed, but none were effective. I slowly began taking painkillers, which gave me a temporary sense of wellbeing. I quickly became addicted, eventually taking a minimum of fourteen a day, double that or more on weekends. I began taking doctor-prescribed Zyprexa and Provigil some time during this period.

2001

My tolerance on painkillers reached its limit. After many tries, I finally quit for good. I returned to addiction support group meetings.

2003

Meds were quickly losing their effectiveness. PTSD symptoms increased in intensity.

2005

I didn't sleep much this year. My hypervigilance and hyperarousal were off the charts. I began feeling the world outside my apartment was "unsafe". My facial features didn't appear stationary when I put make-up on in the mirror. I knew these kinds of thoughts were irrational.

2006

I burned out and witnessed terrifying hallucinations, spirits and/or dark energies in my apartment. I met my future husband, Jack, and quit my job. (I've included an account of this experience after the "About the Author" section.)

2007

I slept as much as I could. I no longer felt the world was unsafe or saw things in my apartment or felt my facial features were moving around on their own. I slowly regained my health.

2008

I began and lost a new job.

2010

I moved in with Jack, and married him.

2011-2012

Since my meds weren't working anymore, I saw no reason to continue them. Very slowly, I began reducing the dosage. By late-

November, 2012, I was drug free for the first time in twenty-five years.

2012-2015

All the original symptoms of my PTSD returned. I tried many alternative healing methods. Almost everything helped, some more than others.

When I reread this outline, I thought, Man, what a horrible life! But I'm highlighting only the PTSD-related elements. I had a variety of jobs. Some were fun and interesting: jazz magazine, bookstores, design galleries. Some were stressful: stock brokerage, managing a realty company. Some were creatively and financially satisfying: advertising, interior designer, marketing manager of design firms. Although I tended to avoid serious relationships and social situations, I was socially adept and met a lot of interesting people. When I felt well enough, I loved to go to movies or out dancing in beautiful clubs. Unfortunately, most of the time, work and PTSD took all my energy and I spent my weekends recuperating.

Shake, Rattle and Roll:
Releasing Buried Energy

December 1, 2012.

My husband, Jack, and I were visiting my uncle in Arizona. I was two days off the anti-depressant I'd been on for twenty-five years. I didn't expect any significant withdrawal symptoms because I'd been lowering the dose in small increments over the course of a year. Plus, I'd had plenty of experience with this kind of thing.

I'd gotten off tranquilizers in my late teens. (In my ignorance, I went cold turkey, which turned out to be a painful mistake. The withdrawal was extremely unpleasant and, due to the nature of benzodiazepines, long-term.)

I quit drinking in my twenties.

I ended a five-year painkiller habit in my early forties. (It took about twenty-eight tries, but I finally did it and good riddance. I'll never forget the withdrawal pain in my legs and bizarre spasms in my arm muscles.)

I got off the anti-psychotic Zyprexa without much difficulty. More difficult was losing the forty pounds I put on with it. (Two-and a half-hour work-outs five days a week, plus limited calories for four months, did the trick.)

I withdrew from Provigil and Concerta fairly easily. The hardest part was losing the jolt of energy they gave me every morning.

I'd been prescribed many other psychiatric drugs over the years, but since most of them proved ineffective, I never stayed on them long enough to experience any withdrawal.

Now, at the age of fifty-five, I was finally, completely drug-free.

I did not do it to be virtuous.

If the meds had continued to do what they'd done for years (allow me to sleep pretty well and keep me relatively balanced), I'd probably still be on them. But, after twenty years, they stopped working. Plus, my prescribing psychiatrist changed. He was suddenly angry all the time and spent our sessions talking so much, I couldn't get a word in edgewise. It was bizarre. Then he'd forget to tell me when he left town, which you can imagine was problematic when I called in for prescription refills. I couldn't count on him anymore.

So there I was in sunny Arizona. I'd visited my uncle many times and was happily familiar with the area. He had a beautiful house on a golf course in a gated-community. I could see Camelback Mountain from his patio. There were hummingbirds and eagles and bunnies and all kinds of wildlife you never saw in Chicago. And then there were the stars at night, billions of them, spread out as far as the eye could see. I never saw anything like that back home. Downtown Chicago was so brightly illuminated, it obscured the light of all but the most brilliant stars.

After we finished dinner that first night, my husband, my uncle and I sat around the kitchen table talking. My uncle began going into painful detail about the last torturous months of my beloved grandmother's life (d. 1977). Then he began talking about the horrors my mother went through when she was dying of cancer (d. 1979), the details of which I knew only too well.

As I listened, I felt a strange, uncharacteristic sensation rising vertically within from my core through to my chest area. It felt something like panic.

Then I felt a coldness in the center of my chest, but it couldn't be environmental. My uncle always kept the house at eighty-two degrees. I began to shiver.

I slipped on my blazer, but still could not stop shaking.

No one noticed.

As if under hypnosis, my uncle continued detailing horrific memories while my husband listened politely.

My shivering accelerated. It was getting out of control. Pretty soon they'd notice. I felt agitated. I couldn't stay seated.

I signaled to Jack I was going out for a cigarette. I walked onto the patio and closed the glass doors behind me.

Blessed silence.

I sat at one of the umbrella tables and lit up.

The air was soft, the golf course dark, the palm trees lining the entrance road dimly lit. I could see the asphalt of the golf cart track just off my uncle's property glistening from the automatic sprinkler system. Soon the bunnies would emerge. When a full moon was overhead, I could see their silhouettes on the fairway.

Everything was still.

Except me. My body would not stop shaking. I kept relaxing my muscles, taking deep breaths, willing myself to stop trembling. I thought I must be getting a cold.

After a while, the shivering stopped and I went back inside. My uncle had gone to bed. My husband and I soon followed.

A few nights later, my cousin and I were driving to pick up a couple pizzas for dinner. We were having a nice time chatting. We'd lived in the same apartment building as kids, but I hadn't see her much after her family moved out of state. She brought up an absurd rumor that had gone the rounds in our family thirty years before. I'd supposedly said something rude, unkind and bigoted to someone who'd married into the family. It was a ridiculous, absurd, twisted lie that caused me considerable pain, especially when I realized so many members of my extended family immediately believed it without question.

As I explained to my cousin what actually happened, that strange cold feeling in my chest opened up and I began to shake again. Shortly after we changed the subject, the shivering dissipated.

I kept waiting for other symptoms of a cold to kick in, but none did.

A couple weeks after we returned to Chicago, Jack and I had family over for dinner.

Sometime after everyone arrived, that cold feeling opened up in the center of my chest again and the involuntary shivering began. Simultaneously, I became drenched in sweat. I told everyone I'd picked up some kind of weird virus out west and hoped it wasn't Desert Fever.

As the weeks went by, I noticed that whenever I spoke about anything from my childhood or on any subject that evoked deep emotion in me, I'd get that cold feeling in my chest and begin shaking. I was mystified.

One night, I began reading *Waking the Tiger* by Peter Levine. He said that when animals in the wild are caught by a predator and are unable to fight or flee, their survival brain automatically puts them into a freeze state. If they somehow escape and reach safety, they automatically, spontaneously shake. This rebalances their system, which had been flooded with stress hormones to deal with their trauma.

Though humans are mammals, too, people are often unable to shake out trauma energy after surviving a mortal threat the way animals do. Over time, if they cannot discharge that energy, they develop symptoms of PTSD.

I went through a four-year period of trauma as a kid. When I was safe again, I was unable to release the trauma energy. I never shook it out. I spent most of the decades that followed in alternating states of dissociation, despair, hypervigilance, hyperarousal, depersonalization

11

(feeling unreal), and derealization (the world feels unreal). Unpleasant, repetitive, intrusive thoughts were frequent. Every so often, I was flooded with rage inappropriate to context. My mid-thirties brought flashbacks. My early forties were rife with night terrors. I tried to kill all this dead with alcohol, tranquilizers, anti-depressants, anti-psychotics, and painkillers (not all at the same time.)

Levine said drugs taken to stabilize your system will buy you time, but when it goes on too long, they interfere with the body's natural rebalancing response and healing.

After reading all this, I sat back on the couch flabbergasted. No therapist or psychiatrist ever explained this to me.

Now I understood what was happening. At long last, my body was releasing trauma energy the way it should have years before.

I was so happy, so optimistic. I thought, *I'll just keep shaking out all that old, frozen, trauma energy and pretty soon, I'll feel whole again—like I did when I was a little girl, before everything went bad.*

Well…it didn't turn out to be quite that simple.

...

P.S. For those interested in knowing if there were any physical side effects after going off Imipramine, there were. I felt random electrical zaps in my head multiple times a day. They were unpleasant and irritating, but only lasted a couple seconds and ended completely after three weeks. I also had hot flashes from my head to my waist and severe cramping on the left side of my back when I laid down to sleep. These side effects also ended after a few weeks. As expected, sleep was a challenge. For the first couple months, I'd often go a night or two without any, but this slowly improved. Very slowly.

The Big Hurt: The Physical Pain of Buried Emotion

After the holidays, I began waking each morning to the feeling of a hundred-pound weight pressing down on my chest. I also felt something pushing down the top of my head. The feeling was so real, I'd slip my hand over my head, sure I must have shimmied up to the wall in my sleep and wedged my head against it, but that was never the case. That didn't concern me as much as the crushing weight on my chest. It felt like a massive tombstone. I found it difficult to push myself up and out of bed, and it certainly wasn't because I was out of shape. I'd been working-out regularly since I was eighteen (for years exercise and music were the only things, besides drugs, that alleviated PTSD symptoms) and weighed the same as I did when I was twenty-two (one hundred twenty-five pounds at five-foot-seven.) Once on my feet, I felt just fine, all invisible weight gone. Still, I'd take my blood pressure. I wanted to make sure I wasn't having a heart attack. It was usually in the normal range or a little above. To be safe, I went to my cardiologist. He found no heart condition. I went to my internist. All tests came back within normal ranges.

One morning, I slowly woke from a deep sleep and opened my eyes to see a holographic image hovering a foot and a half above my chest. It looked like an old, beat-up football with a few decrepit bandages hanging off it. I instantly understood it was my heart. I watched, astonished, as it slowly disappeared.

This really blew my mind. I'd been sent a clear message, but by who or what? It was mindboggling.

For a moment, I felt profoundly sad. This old, beat-up heart of mine had clearly been wounded once upon a time, then kicked around and neglected for years.

Although I'd always had a lot of compassion for others, I'd never had much for myself, which—according to a front-page article in *The New York Times*—is often characteristic to people with PTSD. Since I was a child, I'd always pushed through discomfort and pain without much reflection or meaningful effort to comfort myself (beyond the dubious methods of smoking, drinking and drugging). Seeing a metaphorical image of a beat-up heart projected above my chest, I felt compassion for it. It had suffered abuse while in my care and I had abandoned it. How could I take care of it now, though?

After breakfast, I tried to meditate on all this, but I couldn't focus because my feet were killing me.

The pain was nothing new.

It had begun slowly about five years before. Sometimes my feet burned. Sometimes they buzzed as if being bitten by hundreds of bees. Sometimes they felt like they'd been whipped to shreds. I blocked it out in the beginning, hoping it would go away, which had always been my initial response to any discomfort. Eventually, I did go to a podiatrist, but he found no organic condition to account for it.

These unpleasant sensations were becoming a constant, and either prevented me from falling asleep or woke me from sleep. Anti-inflammatories did nothing. Sea-salt baths and Moisturel moisturizing lotion relieved it for a few hours, but the pain always returned.

The morning I saw my beat-up heart, I decided to give my feet a sea-salt soak. While I ran the bath, I sat on the closed toilet seat and slipped on my iPod earbuds to listen to a sixties playlist I'd recently created. Much to my surprise, I was flooded with staggering grief.

I'd spent thirty years cycling through mild to extreme states of hyperarousal, numbness, hypervigilance, despair and rage—but almost never sadness. I could count on one hand the times I cried over the decades.

Now feelings of intense sadness, abandonment, and loss overwhelmed me. I sobbed like a baby. I cried for my beat-up, neglected heart. I cried for every sad memory that came to mind with every sad song on my sixties playlist. The crying was so out of control, it felt frightening. It almost felt like a kind of vomiting.

Then, finally, after almost an hour, it was over.

I blew my nose, washed my face, brushed my teeth, combed my hair, sat back down and guzzled a bottle of water.

I lit up and then stopped in my tracks.

My feet didn't hurt.

I couldn't believe it.

All the pain was gone.

But more than that, my feet felt delightful—like foam cushions!

Did crying get rid of the pain in my feet? I grabbed my iPhone, did an Internet search, and came upon an article that said when we block out unpleasant emotions, we may think we get rid of them—but we don't. We've only buried them. Apparently, I'd pushed my sadness as far from my heart as it could get.

I was thrilled. I'd found another way to release buried energy.

Between shaking it out and crying it out, I'd be rid of PTSD in no time!

For the next couple months, I woke each morning overwhelmed with sadness. I'd immediately go into the bathroom, put on my iPod, and cry me a river.

Crying continued to feel like throwing up. In fact, I often woke with extreme nausea, which only went away when I cried.

Sometimes, I'd have crying jags a few times a day. I wondered if all the sadness I'd shoved down or blocked out since I was a little girl was coming up now to be felt and released, and if so, exactly how long this process was going to take.

After about two months, the daily deluge slowed to almost nothing. I still cried sometimes. In fact, I was now brought to tears quite easily for any multitude of reasons—a sad movie, the sight of someone else crying, watching sparrows eat the bread I'd throw them. (Go figure on that last one.)

But the daily tsunamis stopped and the pain in my feet never returned.

As Tears Go By:
Releasing Stress Hormones

There was a song in the sixties called "As Tears Go By". I was in grade school at the time. When it came on the radio, my mother sang along and looked very sad, which was unsettling because she always said how happy we all were and I wanted to believe it.

We were a typical alcoholic family. Denial was rampant. My mother and brother either pretended nothing was wrong with my father and/or they dissociated. I knew things were terribly wrong—especially since I was the focus of my father's unpredictable, terrifying alcoholic paranoia and rage—but as long as my mother and brother acted as if everything was great, I was only too happy to go along with them. I wanted to believe! Maybe they knew something I didn't and everything was really okay. Even so, every day after school, I went downstairs into the basement and checked the paint closet where my dad kept his forever-replenished supply of cockroach-brown whiskey pints. I'd empty them halfway and refill them with water. It never helped, never changed him back to the wonderful dad I remembered from long ago.

When your reality is denied over and over as a kid, it can really screw you up later on. Even if you have a genius I.Q., it's difficult and hazardous navigating the world when you've learned to disregard your instincts, ignore your senses and depend on other people to determine your reality. I spent decades depending on other people to tell me what was real. This ingrained habit not only made me feel crazy sometimes, it put me in a lot of dangerous situations—not that danger ever alarmed me. I was generally recessed so far inside me that I didn't feel anything.

Now, well into middle-age, emotions buried long before were emerging. Sometimes it could be overwhelming like when I'd cry and cry and cry. Since I always found the more I understood something, the less powerless I felt, I did a little research on the subject of tears.

There are three kinds: basal, reflex and emotional.

Basal tears are constant. They lubricate your eyes.

Reflex tears protect your eyes from irritants like onions and smoke.

Emotional tears release stress hormones like cortisol and also stimulate a natural painkiller, which is why people usually feel better after they cry.

Because people with PTSD are often flooded with fight-or-flight stress hormones like cortisol, which interfere with a person's ability to sleep, digest, and relax, it is especially good for someone with PTSD to cry when they can, if only to clear out toxic chemicals and prevent inflammation.

I really don't like crying. I always feel better afterwards—body pains, nausea and fatigue lift—but I find it quite unpleasant. I especially don't like the sad memories that often pop up.

I read a fascinating book called *Illumination—The Shaman's Way of Healing* by Alberto Villoldo, Ph.D. He explained "the shaman's way" of processing emotion related to trauma is to experience the raw feeling, but detach from any associated storyline so you are only left with the physical sensation of the emotion.

I found this idea of snipping off the storyline helpful, not only when I felt terribly sad, but also when I became suddenly overwhelmed with anger. If I stepped back from the situation, stopped going over whatever I thought triggered the rage, and simply experienced what it felt like in my body, it quickly dissipated. Then when I was calm again, I found I could think more clearly and determine if there was actually a problem or if I overreacted due to sudden hyperarousal and the flooding of stress hormones.

Of course, easier said than done. Sometimes, the best I could do was realize I was about to go nuts over nothing and back out of the room, saying to Jack, "I'm backing away. I'm backing away." He understood what that meant. I'd back myself into the bathroom, shut the door, sit down and breathe. Other times, I couldn't sit down. I'd practically run to the den, pick up my boxing gloves and start pounding the punching bag.

I always felt so much better when I didn't act out.

I did notice that the more I practiced mindful meditation, the easier it was for me to be aware enough to step away or stop myself before doing or saying something I'd later regret, which leads me to my next chapter.

Hello, It's Me:
Mindful Meditation of the Body

I read a great article in *The Wall Street Journal* called "Brain, Heal Thyself" by Norman Doidge about neuroplasticity and the brain's ability to adapt, change and heal. Capacities formerly thought permanently lost due to conditions like a stroke can sometimes be recovered through exercise of the mind and body.

That got me to thinking about the feedback loops in our bodies and why mindful meditation has been more effective for me than the more traditional methods of focusing on the breath alone.

I've never been the mellow type particularly. In fact, I've been pretty tense since I was about nine.

When my childhood trauma ended, I was a teenager and began drinking. You can imagine how well that went. Black-outs. Waking up in strange places. Jekyll/Hyde behavior and the horrendous remorse that went with it. I quit when I was nineteen and, except for the year I was twenty-four, did not drink again.

I tried marijuana over and over, hoping to experience the same peaceful, easy feeling all my friends did, but it only made me paranoid.

Tranquilizers gave me black-outs worse than alcohol so they were no good.

Amphetamines were never of interest. I wanted to calm down, not amp up. Nor did I ever consider hallucinogens. Between the flashbacks and night terrors I'd known, no way was I going to risk a "bad trip".

The meds prescribed at twenty-nine blanketed my symptoms. They numbed me and allowed me to sleep at night. Keeping a job was easier. (I'd had about fifteen jobs by that time.)

When despair became unbearable in my mid-thirties, I self-medicated with painkillers. Five years later, my tolerance was so great that taking twenty to thirty in a day had no effect, so I quit.

In my late-forties, all psychiatrist-prescribed meds slowly stopped working.

I had to find a way to relax and find the still point within—without pharmaceuticals.

One way I tried was meditation, the kind where you focus on the breath, but I didn't like it. I couldn't sit still doing that for longer than a couple minutes. I'd get nervous, increasingly hyper. For a long time, I thought it was because of my teeny, tiny breaths. I'd start panicking about having smoked for decades and probably having lung cancer, or getting it any minute.

But now I think the reason I got so nervous was because I was almost always in a state of hypervigilance and feeling the need to scan my environment, which I couldn't do when my eyes were closed and I was focusing on my puny breaths.

When I practiced mindful meditation of my body, I was more relaxed and came to enjoy it. I spent so much of my life detached below the neck, not feeling my body at all or feeling as if I were Novocain-ed. It was interesting now to become aware of what was going on down there.

I can frequently find the still point within after I systematically inventory my body for sensation from head to toe. I start with my left foot. I ask myself how it feels, if there is any sense of movement, if it's vibrating, buzzing, burning, pulsating, if it feels squeezed, neutral, numb, light, heavy, cold, hot, if I can feel the air around it, and so on.

I've found that if any spot feels uncomfortable and I stay with it in a relaxed, non-judgmental way, not trying to change it, just feeling the sensation, it will often transform, melt away or disappear. If it becomes too intense, I find a pocket of neutrality or wellbeing in another area and stay there for a while. (This is an example of pendulation—the going back and forth between an uncomfortable experience and a comfortable one—which ultimately serves to undermine the intensity and power of the uncomfortable experience.)

Eugene Gendlin's *Focusing* is a wonderful book which details how to get to the heart of what your body/mind is trying to tell you. Be careful if you have lost blocks of time, though, because body memories, or the metaphorical equivalent of trauma, can suddenly emerge. Go slowly and pull out if it feels too intense or unsafe. All in all, it's an amazing technique that has surprised me time and again with revelations. I had several flashbacks to previous lives while focusing. Given I didn't previously believe in reincarnation, that really blew my mind.

Jack is a pilot. He was taught to mindfully ask himself questions about how he feels before flying to avoid risking an accident from fatigue or stress. Pilots are also supposed to maintain continual situational awareness in the cockpit. If they get fixated on one thing and stop paying attention to any of their instruments, there could be big trouble.

When I am unaware of how I feel physically or emotionally, it seems like my survival brain gets stressed out because it can't upload the information it needs to assess my situation. It's as if the instruments of its cockpit go dark then and it responds by flooding me with stress-hormones to prepare for the worst of all possible scenarios. If I regularly take mindful inventory of how I feel, it seems like my survival brain calms down, understanding I am not in immediate danger.

I often find, after practicing mindful meditation, I have grown quiet inside in the nicest way. According to the theory in the *Wall Street Journal* article, if I practice it often enough, my brain might begin to change and heal.

David Berceli's Trauma Releasing Exercises, which I talk about in another essay, is another method of communicating a sense of safety to my survival brain. I find hot baths effective, too. When I immerse myself in warm water, my body calms down. I think it's an atavistic thing. My survival brain senses I'm safe when I'm in water because in the caveman days, we'd only wash up in the lake when there was no threat, and we were surrounded and protected by our tribe.

Always and everywhere, I'm trying to figure out how to better communicate with my survival brain. I can't use language, because the reptilian and mammalian brains (survival brain) developed before the neocortex (thinking brain). The survival brain just doesn't compute words and thoughts, only the language of the senses. It's a continual challenge that inspires me to be creative.

Strange Things Happen in This World: Frozen Time and Parallel Universes

January, 1998.

I was two days into a new job in downtown Chicago.

I sat stiffly before my computer, pupils dilated, absolutely miserable, wondering how I'd make it through the day. My bones ached. My sinuses were in overdrive. My GI tract was roiling. My lungs felt like they'd been left out in the desert sun for two months and then reinserted. And I was absolutely exhausted, not having slept the night before.

The view outside my window was depressing—the skies dark and gray, the street-snow dirty and condensed, shoved up against the curbs along Wacker Drive. A long fluorescent ceiling bulb one cubicle over blinked uncertainly. The world was colored in drab.

I'd been hired as a marketing manager for a large design firm, a position I'd held previously. There wasn't much to do yet. There were no proposals to write. It was too early in the year for clients to have gotten their project budgets approved. All I could do at that point was familiarize myself with the firm's general marketing material and browse old proposal files.

I felt especially miserable that particular day because my supply of painkillers had been cut off and I was in withdrawal. I'd been taking fourteen every weekday for a year and double that on Saturdays and Sundays. My supplier had been arrested and I'd run out of pills the day before starting this new job.

I knew what lay ahead. I'd withdrawn involuntarily many times.

But something else was happening. Something strange I'd never experienced.

I knew, beyond a shadow of a doubt, that were I to go downstairs and take a cab thirty minutes north to the suburb I grew up in, I'd find my family and my sixteen-year-old self there in the old house as we were in 1972.

Intellectually, of course, I knew this was impossible. But the visceral certainty that this era was co-existing with the present was so overwhelming, so powerful, so undeniably real—it was breaking my heart.

How I longed to see us all there again, to explain to my family who I loved so much what we didn't know back then and to take the action necessary to prevent the tragedies to come. I'd sit my sixteen-year-old self down and explain what had happened when I was little, how the trauma energy had been buried, and how it had affected my body, mind and soul. I'd tell my teenage self I hadn't done anything wrong, I wasn't "evil", that there was nothing inherently offensive about me, and I didn't have to drink myself into oblivion at every opportunity.

This felt-sense of 1972 superimposed over 1998 wasn't a feeling of nostalgia and it was completely different than a flashback. It was unlike anything I'd ever experienced. It was as if somehow the past dimension and the present dimension had become entangled, as if time-lines had been tripped and crossed. And because I could not find the door into this lost world a hair's breadth away, every cell in my being was awash with sadness.

Every day for three weeks, I felt this and then, as mysteriously as it came, the feeling went away. The door had closed.

...

There is a wonderful abstract available on the Internet entitled "Post Traumatic Stress Disorder—What Happens in the Brain?" by Sethanne Howard and Mark W. Crandall, MD. In trauma, when the thinking brain is hijacked by the survival brain and stress hormones flood the body, normal memory integration is often interrupted. Traumatic events do not necessarily get filed away as having passed. They live on in fragmented, disconnected memory bits and the result is that we sometimes viscerally experience the past in the present.

According to that theory, it's possible what I experienced in those three weeks had something to do with unintegrated sense memories which had been triggered by something or other. In the years since, I've read a bit about physics, parallel universes and the concept that all time is now as well as many accounts of those who have had Near Death Experiences who say that once freed of our physical bodies and no longer limited to five senses, we understand that everything happens simultaneously, even our multiple reincarnations. I have no reason to doubt that any or all of this is true, but it's beyond my capacity to understand at the moment. I'm okay with simply accepting what happened in the more quotidian terms related to PTSD, although it's fun to think we could have access to the past, walk right in and set things "right".

I feel fortunate that the few flashbacks I had, the kind where you are hurtled back through time to re-experience original trauma, began and ended in my early thirties and never returned. Maybe they ended for good because I lived each flashback incident through to the end without freezing or dissociating. I'm theorizing, though. I don't really know.

...

One evening, a few months after I got off the meds, Jack and I were in the living room, watching a wonderful old movie on television.

The apartment was fragrant with the smell of a tomato sauce simmering in the kitchen. The city skyline was aglow with the setting sun. The light in the apartment was warm, soft and ambient, the air calm, gentle, and peaceful.

Suddenly, apropos of nothing, I felt the presence of two small girls, four and five years old, standing before me quaking with fear and begging for protection. I couldn't see them, but their reality was so tangible and the energy of their telepathically-transmitted communication so real and true, I had no choice but to react. I felt protective of them and angry at anyone who would terrorize these two small, defenseless children. I leapt to my feet, told Jack what I was experiencing and not to freak out, but I had to address the energy hounding these girls. I pushed them behind me and laid into the perpetrator. I commanded the dark energy terrorizing these children to leave and never come back, nor was it to approach any child again for all of eternity. I also admonished it in no uncertain terms for its unconscionable bullying and abusive behavior. When I finished, it was clear the entity had cleared out. I knew the girls would be safe forever. I fell back on the couch, exhausted but triumphant. It was only then that my mind began to boggle.

What the hell happened?

My husband, God bless him, looked a little more wide-eyed than usual, but he was cool. He'd seen me go through so much in the years we'd been together. I think he assumed I was releasing buried energy in a new, creative way.

When I got up off the couch and crossed the room, I felt the most marvelous sensation in my back.

It was as if I could feel it for the first time in my life.

And it felt glorious! As if it were made of velvet!

That fabulous feeling came and went the next few weeks, each time filling me with a sense of delight, wonder and awe. I knew it had to do with protecting those girls. In having their back, so to speak, I discovered my own.

So what happened? Who were those little girls? Maybe they were soul parts who split off when my trauma was too severe. Maybe they were wandering ghosts and I had a psychic-medium moment. Maybe they were angels helping me release deeply buried energy, which if I hadn't, would have made me sick. Maybe it was a mix of my PTSD-brain's unintegrated, tangled-up memory bits crisscrossing errant dimensions.

Who knows? Sometimes life is just a mystery.

Let's Go Get Stoned:
Painkillers and PTSD

My twenties were a blur of increasing emotional numbness, despair, fatigue, baffling somatic pain no doctor could diagnose, insomnia, short-term, low-paying jobs, and increasing isolation as friendships died off because no one could count on me. I never knew from one day to the next how I'd feel. Sometimes energetic and engaging, but more and more often, numb and lifeless. Planning anything became an effort in futility. I loved being with people when I felt good. But I rarely felt good anymore. Increasingly, I spent my free time alone, demoralized and baffled by how my life was turning out.

I didn't understand why I couldn't fix this. I'd been remarkably resourceful and resilient as a child and teenager. Why couldn't I figure my way out of this? I tried so many things to jumpstart my life. Therapy (when I could afford it), regular exercise, volunteer work, applying the techniques of self-help books, journaling, drawing and painting, acting and dancing classes, religion, research. Nothing made much difference. Not for long. I just kept getting worse.

The summer I was twenty-nine, I was so exhausted and in so much pain, I called in sick to work for a month. Everything ached— my bones, my joints, my muscles, my back, my head. Even my skin hurt. The bottom of my feet were covered with eczema. My left eyelid had fallen to half-mast like Abraham Lincoln's. Night after night, I couldn't sleep. As time went by, it was difficult to speak coherently. Doctors couldn't find anything physically wrong. I was still being diagnosed as a depressive at the time. I sure felt depressed.

Then, one afternoon, I mentioned to someone that my back was killing me and they gave me a painkiller.

It was a Percocet, not that it matters.

I put it in my pocket and went home. It was hot and airless in my apartment that September night. I lay flat on the floor, listening to records. I suddenly remembered the pain pill, took it out of my jeans and drank it down with water. I couldn't imagine it would do anything to alleviate my pain.

I was listening to The Doors that night. I liked to blast it. I remember "Break on Through to the Other Side" was playing when I first felt the Percocet kick.

Words are inadequate to describe the relief I felt.

It was as close to bliss as I'd ever come.

I actually wept with happiness.

What a night it was. It was like a spiritual experience.

And then another miracle. I slept for twelve hours.

...

After that night, I tried getting doctors to prescribe me painkillers giving reasons from back pain to migraines to PMS, but no doctor ever would. I always looked too good, too healthy, no matter how lousy I felt inside. Occasionally, I'd get Vicodin after dental work, but that was it.

About eight years after the first pain pill, I moved into a high-rise downtown and discovered the night-time doorman sold drugs.

At last, I'd found access to a regular supply.

Now that I could feel great whenever I wanted, I could make plans with people. I could have a life. It may have been synthetic wellbeing, but so what. For the first time in years, I felt alive and happy. How I'd missed having fun in my twenties and early thirties.

I especially loved going to The Pump Room at The Ambassador East Hotel (renamed now, under new management). They had jazz trios who played all the old songs from the thirties and forties. I'd dance and eat delicious food in the cushiony, leather booths, watching people, talking with my date or friends, dreaming dreams, enjoying myself. I liked going to the movies, concerts and clubs and going out to eat afterwards. The Coq D'Or in The Drake Hotel was wonderful back then. They had marvelous sliced chicken sandwiches and delicious chocolate ice cream pies. For a brief time there was also a fabulous place called The Gold Star Sardine Bar in a massive pre-war building on Lake Shore Drive. It was a dream jazz club where the music was so out-of-this-world beautiful, I practically cried with joy every time I went. When singers like Tony Bennett were in town, they'd drop in and join the set. It was too good to last, of course, and the club eventually shut down.

You know how this story is going to end.

Slowly but surely, I built up a tolerance so great, no amount of Vicodin, Norco, Percocet, Percodan or Morphine could alter my state of being. For the final year, I took dozens of pain pills every day just so I wouldn't get sick.

Due to the doorman's supplier being arrested so often, I withdrew cold turkey involuntarily about twenty eight times. The last time was my choice. I was tired of spending a small fortune every week just so I didn't go into withdrawal.

I've seen a lot of online forums where people ask how long withdrawal lasts and what you can do to avoid feeling sick

For me, physical withdrawal peaked at seventy-two hours and the worst was over at five days. It was extremely uncomfortable, like having the worst flu on earth, which is why so many people relapse. Unless I took other mind-altering chemicals or prescribed-medications which blocked withdrawal symptoms, there was very little I could do to avoid feeling bad.

In the first twenty-four hours, my sinuses were active, my pupils dilated, and I felt all-over lousy. It was difficult falling asleep and staying asleep. I was very depressed. All I could think about was how much I wanted painkillers.

In the second twenty-four hours, I had diarrhea. Since I smoked so much when I was on drugs, when they were removed, my lungs felt awful. My breathing was shallow and required effort. The bones in my legs started to ache and got worse by the hour. I was incredibly down and obsessed trying to think of any way possible to get painkillers. I felt exhausted, but couldn't sleep. If I laid down, my bicep muscles started to spasm. I tied them up to stop the flip-flop feeling. I also tied up my ankles and knees to dull the pulsing pain there.

These symptoms peeked at seventy-two hours and then slowly receded.

I could drink gallons of water, exercise for hours, take lots of aspirin and hot sea-salt baths, but when my body was in withdrawal, all it would do was scream for drugs and nothing I did significantly calmed it down.

The best advice I ever got was to just accept that you're going to feel really bad for a few days.

But once you're done, that's it—you're done.

For me, support groups were really helpful. I learned how to live life without drugs. (And by the way, you don't have to believe in God to attend 12-step meetings. Take what you can use and leave the rest.)

As of this writing, I am fifteen years off painkillers. I wouldn't go back to them if you paid me. I don't blame myself a bit for taking them, though. My life had been very painful for many years. But painkillers can only be, at best, a short-term solution due to the inevitable increase in tolerance. It can also get expensive and dangerous because they unpredictably depress your breathing mechanism, which is why so many people accidently die taking them.

Lush Life: Why People With PTSD Get Monster Hangovers

I remember reading *Seventeenth Summer* when I was in grade school. I was so excited at the thought of being a teenager, going to high school and dating boys. I can't remember the storyline from that old-fashioned, happy-ever-after novel, but I do know it didn't remotely resemble my seventeenth summer, which was spent drinking all day and night in the Rush Street area of Chicago.

In 1974, five days after I graduated high school, my parents moved from our home in the suburbs to a high-rise downtown. Our apartment was a few blocks from Rush Street, long famous for its bars, nightclubs, jazz joints and, at that time, discos! Although I'd been grounded for the summer, for reasons I cannot remember, there was no one home to keep me from leaving during the day since both my parents worked. Even when they were home on the weekends, they couldn't force me to stay there.

Every morning at a quarter to eleven, I'd leave our apartment and walk down Division Street to meet my best friend at the Clark and Division subway station (now relocated). Though only two blocks from Lake Michigan, I don't remember one cool, balmy breeze that summer—just broiling hot sun. I'd prickle, uncomfortably hot, and then feel the slow trickle of sweat down my chest and under my arms. I'd pass the open doors of Shenanigans, Butch McGuire's, and Mother's and, for a moment, the cool frigid air smelling of spilled beer and Mr. Clean would wash over me. Subway trains rumbled underfoot, sending up billowing waves of dense, dank, urine-scented air through the sidewalk vents. Finally, I'd get to the red-painted bannister at the top of the subway stairs, light up a Marlboro Red and pray my friend arrived soon.

I loved being with my best friend, Dianne. We laughed like crazy that summer, hour after hour, drinking beer in the cool, dark with juke-box tunes blasting behind us. Though I always chose oldies (three for a quarter), other people played the same top-forty songs over and over: "Rikki Don't Lose That Number", "I Shot the Sheriff", "Feel Like Makin' Love", "Rock the Boat", "Taking Care of Business", "Sundown".

I don't think I ever again laughed as much as I did those days with dear Dianne.

But I sure didn't feel like laughing when I stood waiting for her those late summer mornings. I'd feel almost as awful as I did when I first woke.

To say I "woke" after a night of drinking isn't quite accurate. Two hours after I passed out (after seventeen hours of non-stop drinking), I'd startle awake into a state of visceral terror and panic—my heart hammering, my head pounding, my bladder full to bursting, my GI track roiling, my mouth dry as dust, my hands shaking, my nerves jangling, every cell in my body screaming, "Emergency! Run! Run! Run!"

Though I quit drinking decades ago, I remember those hangovers as if they were yesterday. I never understood how so many alcoholics could drink into mid-life or later when the hangovers were so awful.

Until now.

The physiology of people with PTSD is different than those without it.

PTSD people tend to have high levels of stress hormones like cortisol in their systems. High levels of cortisol affect you in the following ways.

You can't sleep well, so you're tired and wired.

Your adrenal glands are depleted, so you're exhausted.

Cortisol bumps up insulin, drops your blood sugar, and gives you cravings for a quick fix to lift you. That's one reason why a hair of the dog sounds so good the morning after.

Cortisol increases your body's sensitivity to pain, like back and muscle aches, by increasing levels of prolactin, and it also causes headaches by hyper-sensitizing your brain. Even the slightest twinge excites your nerves.

Cortisol increases the secretion of acid in your stomach, causing nausea, heartburn, abdominal cramps, diarrhea, or constipation.

It gives you the jitters, feelings of panic, and even paranoia.

It suppresses feel-good hormones like serotonin and dopamine, so you feel depressed.

It raises your blood pressure and sets your heart to racing.

It interferes with memory integration. (Black-out!)

Hmmm…sounds an awful lot like a hangover to me.

Add to this the fact that alcohol increases cortisol in the body and it's clear why someone with PTSD is going to get a terrible, terrible hangover. Alcohol also dehydrates, due to its diuretic effects. And the more dehydrated you are, guess what? The higher your cortisol.

Anyone who gets drunk is going to get some kind of hangover.

But people with PTSD get hangovers from hell.

Help! How Your Body Reacts to Terror

This is what happens when your body/mind registers a threat to its survival:

The amygdala, part of the survival brain, takes control and shuts down the thinking brain because there is literally no time for thought. It's kill or be killed.

Short-term memory, concentration and rational thought are no longer accessible.

Heart pumps blood to arms and legs so you are able to fight or run. Sometimes this extra blood pressure can be so great, you shake.

You breathe faster so your muscles have the extra oxygen necessary to survive.

Stress hormones like epinephrine and cortisol flood your system, giving you extraordinary strength and power. You've heard of mothers lifting cars off their children. These are the stress hormones that give them super-powers.

Your pupils dilate so you can view a wider panorama.

Your mouth goes dry as fluids are diverted to areas where they are needed most.

Mechanisms normally under frontal lobe control, like holding in urine, are overridden by the survival brain. It is therefore possible you have an accident.

Your survival brain will not allow you to digest because there's no time for that! You are in crisis mode. Instead, you have diarrhea, constipation, nausea, or butterflies.

Your immune system takes a break to reorganize, making it more likely you will get sick if the crisis goes on too long.

Most people, after a short-term crisis, are able to release the trauma energy and return to pre-trauma equilibrium.

Not so for people with PTSD who, for whatever reason, are unable to release the energy after the trauma is over and so develop symptoms over time.

I'm practically exhausted just reading this. When you think that so many of us have spent a lifetime going through this again and again, well…all I can say is we sure are tough.

Crazy: When You Feel Like Killing Someone Because There Is Fruit Residue on the Underside of Your Kitchen Cabinet Knobs

When I was a little girl, my parents took my brother and me to The Pheasant Run Resort in St. Charles, Illinois. (The town also was home to the great Brian Wilson of The Beach Boys for a little while, although not when I was there. Sigh.)

Pheasant Run was brand new and chic when it first opened. It had an indoor replica of New Orleans' Bourbon Street and a big indoor-outdoor pool divided by glass. You could swim under the glass to reach the other side, which was super cool to a kid.

One afternoon, I was frolicking in the pool, splishing and splashing, bobbing up and down, when who do I see standing in the game room parallel to the indoor pool but Gene Rayburn!!

Gene Rayburn was the host of *The Match Game*, a popular game show I used to watch when I was home sick from school.

I was so excited to see him. I waved enthusiastically.

And he waved back!

Boy-oh-boy, was I thrilled.

In *The Match Game* of the sixties, non-celebrity contestants tried to match answers with their celebrity team member to fill-in-the-blank questions.

I played a different kind of Match Game all my life. Unschooled as to how PTSD affected me, my thinking brain always tried to make sense of my hyperarousal by blaming it on people or events, usually in my immediate environment.

I'd walk out on jobs, break up with boyfriends, quit school, cancel plans, stop hanging out with a friend or group of friends, write and mail letters that never should have been mailed (especially those written at three in the morning), fire people, start screaming…the list goes on. Later, when the stress hormones re-balanced and my nervous system settled down, I was often filled with remorse and regret, depending on how inappropriate and extreme my behavior. Sometimes it felt like I was crazy.

Because I lived a pretty isolated life, and only lived with someone briefly after college, I wasn't aware that I almost always assumed that the way I felt inside was because someone else was doing something wrong—usually, I felt, to me.

Once I moved in with Jack, I became embarrassingly aware of how frequently I slipped into fight-or-flight behavior and blamed it on him (or low-stress or even neutral factors in my environment.)

Here are a few of examples of what I've gone nuts over:

The underside of the kitchen cabinet knobs sticky with residue. (Because Jack didn't wash his hands after handling the fruit and touched the knobs!)

Jack bought an extra Lotto ticket. (Not in the budget!)

Jack didn't push in the computer chair when he was done using it, so when I passed through that area, I had to push it in myself. (He doesn't give my welfare a thought!)

Jack didn't replace the paper towel roll after using the last sheet. (He thinks I'm going to pick up after him? Ha!)

And so on.

You get the picture.

None of these scenarios warranted a crazy stressed response, but flooded with stress hormones, my survival brain pushed for discharge, and my thinking brain did the best it could to justify that sense of overwhelm. Although acting-out did temporarily release energy, it was never a healing discharge and always caused me distress later to think I'd needlessly upset Jack.

As time went by, I became more aware of how I felt stress-wise, which allowed me to pause a moment before over-reacting and think something along the lines of, *The context here doesn't equate with the rage I am feeling. It feels like it does, but it's also possible I'm just flooded with stress hormones. Maybe I'll step away. If it still bothers me when I'm calm, I can bring it up and be more articulate.*

This is very difficult to do sometimes when fight-or-flight energy begs for immediate action.

Sometimes the best I can do is say to Jack, "I'm flooded" (he knows what that means), back out of the room and go hit our punching bag for a few minutes. That helps tremendously. Other times, I go into the bathroom and sit on the closed toilet seat and just take a few minutes to quiet down. Hyperarousal fades pretty quickly if I don't feed it with false data.

That's not to say people don't do lousy or annoying things sometimes. My lovely husband does indeed handle the kitchen-cabinet doorknobs with fruit-residue fingers sometimes, but he does not do this to annoy me. He's just so relaxed all the time, he zones out, daydreams, and doesn't pay attention.

Oh, to be so relaxed!

Feelings:
My Key Code for Somatic Pain

I honestly thought I was home free after I cried away the pain in my feet. I really believed I'd released all the sadness I'd unconsciously buried since I was nine.

And I did feel quite fine for a few months, until I strained a gluteal muscle while violently returning tennis balls lobbed by a tennis ball machine in our health-club facilities downstairs. I loved hitting those balls. It felt good no matter what, but especially when I felt angry about anything. I only felt a slight twinge that first night, but hours later I felt terribly nauseous. The next day, my right gluteal maximus was pulsating with pain.

Assuming it was a torn muscle, I treated it like one—icing it on and off for forty-eight hours and staying off it for eight weeks. Certain it was gone, I tried walking at my normal pace again only to find that awful pain instantly returned. I couldn't believe it. Again, I iced it and stayed off it for weeks. Once I felt sure it was thoroughly healed, I carefully went back to slow walking.

Boom! It was back again. Over and over, this happened.

It was so frustrating. Exercise had always been vital to my staying balanced.

Over time, the butt pain somehow spread and then the other side of my butt hurt, though I hadn't strained it that I was aware of. Then my tailbone started bothering me. It felt unbearably tender. What the heck?

I made an appointment with the first of several doctors. The only diagnosis I ever got was chronic gluteal strain, but for reasons I go into another time, I'm not sure this was necessarily true.

I began to notice that my pain, whether caused by an organic condition or not, was often metaphorically significant. (Louise Hays writes interesting books on the metaphysical causes of illness.) The following is my body's key code thus far.

TMJ:

I had TMJ a lot in my thirties. I think of those as my angry years. When I had TMJ, which I found excruciatingly painful, I was keeping my mouth shut and not saying what I wanted and needed to say to certain people. I clenched my jaws shut in my sleep and waking life in order to keep everything inside, particularly rage. I felt so angry all the time, I wanted to scream. I'd pace back and forth, back and forth, whenever I stood waiting for the train. I think I looked a little crazed.

Lower back pain:

I can usually tie this pain to a sudden felt-loss of support, either financial or personal. I might also feel betrayed or stabbed in the back.

Butt pain:

My body is telling me, "You can no longer sit on the pain you've sat on all your life! Out with it!"

Tail bone pain:

When my tail bone feels unbearably tender, I am usually feeling isolated or alienated from or rejected by my "tribe" (primary blood family). When tail bone tenderness spreads into the area on either side of it, I am feeling my most painful childhood feelings, particularly shame, abandonment, anguish, loneliness, powerlessness, and vulnerability.

Foot pain:

This is sadness I pushed as far from my heart as I could get it.

Stomach pain:

Although people with PTSD often develop stomach pain as a result of spending so much of their lives in states of fight, flight, or freeze, and therefore have GI tracts that can't regularly digest food anymore, I've had difficulty "digesting" certain information, especially in relation to how people I've loved treated me. I've often felt like I have a big, square brick in my stomach and it hurts.

Solar plexus pain:

Very old, very deeply buried sorrow. I also feel pain here when my reality has been denied and/or I've lost or feel like I've lost my personal power.

Heart pain:

Sometimes I've literally felt like an arrow has pierced my heart when someone I love has consciously done something hurtful to me, usually family members.

Pressure on my chest: (Please always see your doctor first for any physical issues, particularly regarding the heart.)

Pressure on my chest has sometimes meant I need to get something "off my chest" or that I feel weighted down by my responsibilities or what I have to do, or the pressure I'm under is too great. When I first got off the meds and felt like there was a tombstone on my chest in the mornings, I came to believe the metaphor there was that I was coming back to life after being buried alive by drugs for decades. (Pressure on your chest can also mean ghosts or spirits are trying to communicate, but that's another kettle of fish.)

Weak hands and weak arms:

When my arms and hands feel weak, it means I don't feel capable of handling the situation I'm dealing with, I can't keep carrying the load, I can't be anyone's "right arm". This brings feelings of childhood fear: If I'm not watching everything, protecting and taking care of everyone, my world will fall apart.

Face and other body parts feel like they are thawing out:

The emotional energy that froze in the original trauma is being released or is ready for release. (I go into this more in my essay on visiting an energy healer.)

Migraines:

I haven't got migraines in years, but I remember them well. I used to get them when I was overwhelmed with stress and having trouble keeping threatening emotions down, especially trying not to explode with anger and frustration.

Swollen tongue and sinus trouble:

I have tears to shed and they are piling up.

Nausea:

This means my body is overwhelmed with sadness. I need to cry. I need to get rid of the cortisol.

Fatigue unrelated to sleep deprivation or physical exhaustion:

I get this incredible fatigue out of nowhere and need to lie down immediately, but then I can't sleep. I hate that. I've come to learn this means my body has exhausted its resources trying to keep my sadness in. If I cry, the fatigue lifts.

Neck and head feel like they're being pushed down:

I get this when I've gone too long with tremendous, unrelieved stress. My body is trying to pull itself in like a turtle withdrawing into its shell to protect itself.

Head and/or butt feels clawed:

I can't help but think the feeling of clawed flesh means my original trauma is up for release because I associate tiger claws with Peter Levine's *Waking the Tiger* and his inspiration for Somatic Experiencing.

A shaman gave me the following interpretations to account for pain or discomfort in your fingers:

Thumb: Worry

Forefinger: Fear

Middle finger: Anger

Ring finger: Sadness

Pinkie: Trying. You're making an effort, maybe even trying to force something and it's not necessarily working.

...

Feelings, nothing more than feelings. Remember that song? Turned out feelings weren't so easy to dispose of as I thought when I was young. I believed when I "blocked them out" as a child, they were gone for good. It gave me such a great sense of control, even power. I didn't know energy doesn't disappear, it only transforms. In my case, it laid low for decades and then manifested in physical pain. Although crying got rid of my foot pain, I was having trouble bringing that kind of release to the new pains showing up.

It was time to take unprecedented action.

I made an appointment to see a shaman.

Bless the Beasts and the Children: My Visit to the Shaman

A few months after I got off all meds, my brother gave me some old family photos of me from toddler-stage through my twenties. I showed these to Jack and said it was a strange thing, but whenever I'd seen them—I never identified myself with them, never saw the girl in the photos and thought, "That's me!" It was always as if I were looking at a stranger.

Around the time I told this to Jack, I began waking up in bed in the morning and having the indescribably bizarre feeling of the left side of me being the size of someone who was eight or nine. My left hand felt tiny compared to my right. My left leg felt much shorter than the other. Of course, I was the same size I was normally, but the visceral sense of this impossible reality was disconcerting.

I also began having the feeling of missing all those girls I once was, the ones I saw in the pictures, but couldn't identify with.

I particularly missed those from the ages of nine through sixteen. They felt so physically close in real-time that it was frustrating not to be able to actually see them, talk to them, give them all hugs. The best I could do was write individual letters telling them how much I missed them, how much I admired them, and asking them to come back. I didn't know how to access the mail system of non-ordinary reality, so I just burned the letters after I wrote them.

Not long after, I came across the book *Soul Retrieval—Mending the Fragmented Self* by Sandra Ingerman.

She said when a person, child or adult, is in the midst of trauma and her soul (vital essence, essential self—whatever you want to call it) senses it cannot survive the ordeal, part of it will split off and go somewhere else. As time goes by, the person who survived the trauma doesn't feel like themselves anymore. It feels like some core part of them is missing. They may become chronically depressed and try to substitute drugs or adrenalin-seeking behavior for the lost self. They may become suicidal or physically ill. When the soul or spirit completely leaves, the person goes into a coma.

Maybe soul loss explained the emptiness I'd felt so much of my life. Maybe it accounted for the felt-lack of internal continuity, the sense of having somehow been cut off or separated from my former chronological selves, the disconnect I felt when looking at old photos of me.

Theoretically, a shaman can journey to places in non-ordinary reality where soul parts have gone and bring them back to you, blowing them into the appropriate chakra(s). Sometimes they find your younger selves held fast in a moment of old trauma, encapsulated, frozen in time—waiting to be set free and reunited with you.

Although I accepted other people's versions of reality over my own for many years, I learned the hard way that those people were not infrequently wrong. By denying my own reality—ignoring my instincts, the feedback of my senses, my direct perception, the rational conclusions of my not inconsiderable intellect—I began a process that resulted in almost total self-destruction.

The idea of going to a shaman, getting my soul parts back, and feeling whole again was beyond wonderful. As always, I did my research. I read a lot of books on shamanism by Alberto Villoldo, Michael Harner and others.

While searching for a shaman, I did a lot of mindful meditating.

It had become much easier with daily practice to fall into a Theta-brainwave state. (Brainwaves are synchronized electrical pulses produced by masses of neurons communicating with each other. There are four types differentiated by frequency: Beta = alert, Alpha = relaxed, Theta = deeply meditative or between sleep and wakefulness, Delta = sleep.)

I also began visualizing a lovely, safe place in my imagination before sleeping. As time went by, I noticed I wasn't alone in that beautiful place. Eventually, I saw what appeared to be thirteen of my split-off soul parts. Most were under fourteen. Two looked like a generic-me in my early twenties, but seemed to have no other role than to protect the younger selves. (This was not Multiple Personality Disorder, which is the most severe form of dissociation. The younger selves I saw appeared to be parts who'd left at moments of high trauma so the chronological-me could survive.) I also saw my mother and other deceased female relatives. Everyone was always having a lovely time together. I talked to all my younger selves and asked if they'd consider returning. Although they appeared to like me a lot, they seemed content to stay where they were. I didn't blame them. My fifty-something self wasn't having much fun given the exhaustion and pain I'd been experiencing.

I'd begun to wake up feeling overwhelmingly nauseated, so much so I'd immediately put my head between my legs or move low to the floor in case I passed out. I avoided leaving the house for fear I'd faint or toss my cookies in transit. Even when I felt healthy, what fun was there for my younger selves to enjoy? I didn't play or color, ride bikes or horses. I didn't have dolls or kid games. My teenage selves loved to drive and blast tunes, but I hadn't had a license in thirty years. Why should they come back?

Of course, it was a possibility I was imagining all these little Ann E. Lauries. But if I wasn't, and I found a true shaman who could journey into non-ordinary reality and convince my soul parts to come back home to me, I would know because I'd feel significantly different afterwards. Better. More substantial. More whole. More me!

I went online and found three shamans advertising their services in the Chicagoland area. Two were in the suburbs and one downtown. I chose the latter.

I checked into her background. She had a post-graduate degree from a good university. She'd studied energy work and shamanism under "many teachers". That was a little ambiguous, but the fact that she'd been doing this for twenty years gave me some confidence. The cost of a soul retrieval was $120. If she was for real, that wasn't much to pay.

I called for an appointment.

I cabbed it over one sunny, summer afternoon. She had a small storefront with an art gallery in front and a healing space in back. It was dark inside. The shades were drawn, the air calm, still and quiet—smelling faintly of incense. She was barefoot and relaxed, dressed in soft cotton, sitting crossed-legged across from me. She had short hair and wore no make-up. She gave off an intense sixties vibe and I suspected she was a teenager back then.

We talked a while. She asked me a lot of personal questions. If I were to do it again, I wouldn't give her so much information. According to the books I've read, a real shaman can find your soul parts without any autobiographical details about your life.

I laid down on a raised padded table for the ritual. I heard the shaking of rattles before she called her spirit guides and spirit animals to her side with song and dance. I could see her background in the performing arts. Her ritual of calling the spirits was quite beautiful, so streamlined, balletic and flawless, it was almost like a professional performance. She imitated a dolphin and bear in her dance. I can't remember if they merged with her spirit or she merged with theirs, but they all got together somehow.

Then she sat quietly for twenty minutes journeying to the Lower, Middle and Upper Worlds looking for my soul parts. I lay relaxed with open heart, calling my younger selves back to me.

I'd done my own preparation before I arrived that day. I'd asked my guardian angels, spirit animals, spirit guides, and my deceased mother and grandmother to come with me to the appointment to assist the shaman. I figured even if she proved to be a fake, the ritual could still be effective because of my intent and the help of those in spirit I called upon to accompany me.

When the shaman found my soul parts, she blew them into the chakras at the top of my head and into my heart. The instant she did, I felt quite wonderful. I honestly felt a beautiful energy flow through me.

Something had happened.

I just didn't know what.

I sat up and we talked. She said she'd found three of my soul parts—aged nine, sixteen and twenty-two.

I thought, *Three? What about the other ten!!*

I said, "Didn't you find any more?"

She paused, and then said there were a bunch of residual parts hovering around me and they slipped back in, too.

I instinctively felt that response was improvised.

The shaman told me why each soul part left. She was right about why the sixteen-year-old would have taken off, but then she said I wanted to marry the guy I was in love with in high school and she couldn't have been more wrong. I never even remotely entertained the idea of marriage back then, to him or anyone. In fact, for most of my life, marriage sounded like a living hell to me. I told her she was wrong about the marriage part. She smiled and insisted I did want to get married to the guy in high school. It was quite alienating for her to say that. Not only was it false and who would know better than me, but I really, really, really hate it when people deny my reality.

Then she said my nine-year old self split off because of the death of someone named Jamie. I told her I never knew anyone named Jamie or anyone who died until I was twelve.

I sure hoped she hadn't blown the wrong kid back into me.

She also brought back my twenty-two-year-old self. I felt the shaman made that one up based on my telling her that's when my mother died.

I left the shaman a little worried about my other soul parts still out there, particularly those aged three to thirteen. They were the ones who'd suffered the most.

But in spite of the shaman being wrong in some of her interpretation, the actual ritual and experience of having soul parts blown back in felt wonderful. Maybe she did bring in the soul parts she said she did, but was terrible at interpretation. Or it could have been my spirit guides did the work. I don't know, but as a result of the experience, I left feeling better.

When I came home, I sat down alone as directed, and asked the three soul parts who'd theoretically returned the following. Why did you leave? What would make you stay? What would make you happy? I listened for the answers and wrote them down. I was to do this every day for thirty days, and make sure to do the things that would make them happy and stay.

That first night, just as I was falling asleep, I felt a ball of energy fly into my heart chakra.

My eyes flew open.

Then another energy ball flew in.

And another!

I was stunned, absolutely shocked.

I sat up, wide awake. What the heck was happening?

I'd never read anything like that happening after a soul retrieval.

I didn't know much about chakras. I couldn't feel them or see their colors. I didn't work with them in meditation at that point. I knew where they were located, but only had a basic understanding of what they represented. Having energy balls fly into them was an unprecedented and incredible feeling. Nothing extraordinary happened in the hours or days after, but somehow, in some ineffable way, I knew it was a marvelous thing to have happened.

...

Looking back, I still don't know exactly what occurred with that shaman, but I do know the experience was somehow healing.

I felt more joy in simple things. The world appeared fresher, more beautiful, colors more intense. I felt very hopeful and had a sense that surprising and wonderful things could happen at any moment. I also felt an old familiar ache in my legs, the one that used to wake me at night when I was little. My mother called it growing pains. And for a while, a dimple appeared high on my right cheek. I hadn't seen that on my face since I was twelve.

Sometimes I felt an old sadness, too. A feeling like my heart was going to break.

Maybe that sadness was too overwhelming when I was a girl, but I was an adult now. I was strong enough to feel. I could handle it.

It was safe.

It's Only a Paper Moon:
The Matrix and the PTSD Brain

I didn't get around to watching *The Matrix* until 2014. What a great movie. I've watched it three times since and have it saved on my TV recordings.

For the eleven people who haven't seen the movie, "the matrix" refers to a digital reality programmed into people's brains giving them the impression they are walking around in the real world, living authentic, autonomous lives when, in fact, they are living out their entire existence floating in little red pods filled with disgusting viscous fluids, providing energy to machines who virtually control their reality.

The concept of the simulated reality of *The Matrix* reminded me of the PTSD survival brain which so frequently downloads a false sense of reality.

Sometimes my survival brain interprets benign situations as dangerous. Stress hormones flood as my thinking brain goes dark, and I'm off in a state of fight-or-flight. I might go nuts over something trivial or have a panic attack. Maybe I'll freeze, dissociate and involuntarily recede inward. I'll cancel all plans and stay home with my back to the wall and a view of the room's entrance, feeling paralyzed and vaguely afraid. Maybe I'll feel paranoid and imagine significant others are trying to screw with my head. I've gone nuts many times, obsessively trying to manage threatening situations which did not exist, but when stricken with the visceral certainty they did, I manufactured problems to make sense of my body's crisis mode.

My thinking brain is always trying to make sense of the world. That's its job, but with a PTSD-affected survival brain as a partner, that doesn't always work so well. My survival brain is always trying to help me, keep me alive against a perceived threat, but instead it often just makes my life more difficult, reflecting a reality that doesn't exist.

I've found it very difficult sometimes living with two conflicting realities inside: what I feel is true and what I know is true.

Over time, mindful meditation of my body's internal state has helped me navigate more safely through the minefield of fight-or-flight impulses. Now I can do a quick body scan that gives me a level of awareness I didn't have before. I might feel a sense of urgency—heart racing, extremities cold, muscles tense, breathing fast and shallow—but I'll recognize it is a non-sequitur response to actual events. I'll understand my survival brain is sensing a reality that doesn't reflect real-time conditions. I can pause, step back, and not act on the feeling. Not that I always do, since the state of fight-or-flight is so intense, so red hot screaming while my rational brain, telling me to calm down, speaks in a much softer, quiet voice.

In *The Matrix*, Morpheus suggests to the hero, Neo, that there's a chance to win against The Matrix because the machines are governed by a limited set of rules, but since a human being has access to infinite imagination, he can transcend those rules. Neo can create his own reality, one that The Matrix cannot necessarily predict or destroy.

I found this inspiring.

If I learn the rules of my PTSD survival brain, observe and understand how it functions and manifests in my body/mind, I might be able to use my I.Q., my imagination and those of others' to transcend its regime.

One symptom I've desperately wanted to undermine the strength of has been hypervigilance.

I haven't felt safe at my core since I was a little kid. Some part of me has been on alert for decades. Falling asleep was always a challenge as was staying asleep. Usually, I could fall asleep at dawn, although there were periods when I wouldn't sleep for two or three days at a time.

I became so tired of being exhausted.

I wondered how I could transcend my poor survival brain's near-constant sense of emergency. How could I get the message to it that everything was okay and no one was trying to kill me? Unlike the thinking brain, the survival brain literally does not understand words because it evolved before language was invented. It only understands the senses. That's why talk therapy had almost no effect on my PTSD symptoms. It was the survival brain that had to be engaged.

Shamans put themselves into a very relaxed, deeply meditative Theta brain state by a variety of means, including breath work. A common method used is to inhale slowly for seven counts, hold seven, exhale seven, hold seven, and repeat seven times. They usually advise inhaling through the nose and exhaling through the mouth.

A chiropractor told me that one way to immediately interrupt a state of fight-or-flight was to inhale deeply and hold my breath for five or ten seconds. He said this instantly refocuses the survival brain and stops it from maintaining the hyperarousal. Additional breath-work he advised was inhaling for four quick counts, holding four, exhaling four, holding four and repeating as needed.

My step-great granddaughter was advised by her therapist to calm down her survival brain by walking and watching her feet while she walked. Her survival brain literally sees she isn't trapped. She can walk, run, or fight if she needs to—and then it calms down.

In an online forum, a lot of people suggested the practice of looking for five items of one color in the room, then five of another color, and so on—to pull yourself back into the here and now.

I like sea salt baths to soothe myself. I think it's partly an atavistic thing. In caveman days, we'd only feel safe bathing if we were with our tribe and there were no wild animals or warring people in the area. Maybe it's a womb thing, too. Also, sea salt is supposed to draw out toxicities. (FYI, it does not raise your sodium levels.)

I read an article about a woman who sought professional help for insomnia. In her therapy sessions, the therapist would repeatedly toss a ball to her, calling out which hand she should catch it in. The idea was to confuse her right and left brains, which are connected to the right and left hands.

I also came across something called Binaural Beats—audio tracks that theoretically calm down your brain by slowing its frequency.

In 1839, a physicist named Heinrich Wilhelm Dove discovered the signal of our brains could be changed from one state to another by listening to the sounds of different frequencies in each ear. In trying to reconcile the difference between the two frequencies, the brain creates a median signal called a binaural beat.

I did a search on iTunes for "Binaural Beats" and downloaded the first album I came across. Most of the musical pieces were serene. A couple sounded like the soundtrack to some esoteric space movie, which I found sort of alienating. Other cuts included sounds of rain, birds and nature. I found it effective in calming me down when I was hypervigilant, especially at night when my emergency-mode was revving up. (I tend to get tense beginning at five p.m., just like when I was a kid anticipating the night to come.) Late at night, I get sleepy if I turn on the TV with captions, mute it, and play the Binaural Beats while reading the screen.

These are a few of the methods I'm using to disarm "The Matrix" until the entire thing can be dismantled and a new world is born.

Is That All There Is? My Experience with Craniosacral Therapy

I met someone once who went to a craniosacral therapist regularly and pretty quickly was rid of most of her PTSD symptoms, so I did some research.

The craniosacral system (CS) consists of the membranes and fluid surrounding the brain and spinal cord, which extend from the bones of the skull to the tailbone. An imbalance in this area causes sensory motor and/or neurological disabilities. Theoretically, craniosacral therapy can rebalance the system and return it to a pre-trauma state of equilibrium.

The craniosacral system has the equivalent of a cardiovascular pulse. Skilled CS therapists assess the patient's craniosacral rhythm and remove any restrictions they detect with the slight pressure of their fingertip(s) at various locations on the body. The patient doesn't have to take off her clothes or do anything but relax and lie there while the therapist performs her magic.

I chose a nearby CS therapy clinic and made an appointment one winter day. I bundled up in my Air Force Parka (circa 1968) and walked against the battering wind, feeling somewhat hopeful I might get PTSD relief, given my friend's spectacular results. The clinic was on the second floor of a three-story walk-up off Chicago Avenue. The place had a New Age vibe. Instrumental music played softly on hidden stereo speakers. The residue of sweet-smelling incense hung in the air.

The receptionist called my therapist to announce my arrival. She came out and introduced herself. Although she couldn't have been more than thirty, she reminded me of a hippie from back in the day. No make-up, maxi-dress, long, thick, naturally curly hair, very laid-back. She talked in a too-quiet voice, which was a drag because, although I wear hearing aids and read lips, only 40% of all words can be lip-read, so I had to strain to understand her. When I explained my hearing loss and asked her to please speak up or face me when she spoke, she consistently did not.

She led me into a room with red brick walls, a window facing another building and a massage table. She laid a light blanket over me and said we could talk while she worked or I could just relax and even sleep. I certainly wasn't going to try having a conversation with her. The hour would have consisted of me lifting my head off the table over and over, saying, "What? Pardon me? Can you repeat that?"

I laid back and meditated while she lightly pressed her fingertips against various areas from the back of my skull down to my ankles. It was pleasant and tranquil, largely due to the fact that I meditated the entire time.

I felt no change in symptoms during or after the session.

I went back a second time. It was again a serene experience, but afterwards she spoke so ignorantly about PTSD, while claiming great expertise, that I was flabbergasted. I thought if she pretended to expertise in PTSD, then maybe she pretended to expertise in craniosacral therapy, too.

I felt I just couldn't trust her. Plus, there was no change in my symptoms and I didn't have money to burn.

I did not return.

If I had money burning a hole in my pocket and someone I knew highly recommended a craniosacral therapist in Chicago, I would definitely give it a try again.

Kind of a Drag:
The Demoralization of Dissociation

Brain scans show the survival brain lights up during trauma and the thinking brain goes dark. The survival brain interprets the world only through the senses, not through words, so when you look back at the scene of a trauma and ask yourself why you didn't respond in such and such a way instead of how you did, it is in part because your brilliant I.Q. and verbal skills weren't accessible, or were significantly less accessible. When your body/brain believes you are about to die, instinct kicks in, not intellect. Thinking takes too long when annihilation is imminent!

Dissociation is involuntary.

There are many forms and degrees of dissociation. Daydreaming is the most common and benign form. Everyone does it. Multiple personality disorder is at the other end of the spectrum.

When I dissociate, it feels, in retrospect, as if some core part of me recedes so deeply inside that all sensation is blunted as if I'm surrounded by a thick, impermeable synthetic-like shield. For me, this most often happens when significant others behave inappropriately or in a cruel or abusive manner. I'll see what's happening. I'll hear it. I won't black out. But in some intangible way, it simply isn't happening. It isn't real. My survival brain has taken me out of the equation and, therefore, I don't react.

Sometime later—it could be a week, it could be a decade—I'll remember the abusive event sharply, as if it just happened for the first time, and feel utterly demoralized I didn't react and respond to the injustice in the moment.

For years, I didn't understand it. I'd always been known as fearless. I certainly had no problem being effective and articulate in any capacity at work. No one intimidated me in the workplace. Yet when significant others behaved inappropriately, I'd act as if it didn't happen and later, when no longer in a dissociated state, feel pathetic and weak for not effectively responding when the original situation played out.

Sometimes then, I'd obsessively go over and over the incident, imagining articulate and devastating responses that would have stopped the abuse dead, so I would never forget and it could never, ever happen again.

But it would happen again.

Finally, I learned that my survival brain picks up the markers of an abusive situation before it manifests and therefore, before I'm conscious of it, shuts off my thinking brain, and slips me into dissociation. Only when my survival brain senses I am safe, am I able to accurately assess and feel what happened when I was locked inside, so to speak.

It was never the case I lacked courage or intellect. It was just that my body/mind never rebooted after the childhood trauma years, my system never discharged, so I continued to dissociate again and again. Sometimes I've felt as if my survival brain went insane, seeing danger everywhere when there was none, like some kind of Don Quixote character—fighting windmills to protect me, my honor, my life.

Poor dear survival brain. Never one quite so true.

Knock Three Times (or Five or Seven): The Tapping Solution (Emotional Freedom Technique)

I've been in a state of constant fatigue for decades. When I worked, that distracted me, but after losing my job in the recession of 2008, I was home most of the time. The good news was I could take naps whenever I wanted. The not-so-good news was that I didn't fall asleep for daytime naps much better than I did falling sleep at night.

Mid-afternoons, I'd feel absolutely exhausted and go into the bedroom, close the door, pull down the shades, remove my hearing aids, lie down under a light blanket, and feel certain, given my overwhelming fatigue, that I'd surely slip into oblivion instantly, but no—I'd feel too uncomfortable. I'd almost always feel weird, disconcerting pockets of energy vibrating all over the place inside. Almost always, the bottom of my feet pulsed as if I were standing on the floor of a huge, industrial factory running at full-speed. There was usually energy moving up and down my left calve as if cells were taking elevators to different floors in my leg. My chest area tended to be very active with chaotic movement. I could almost visualize fireworks going off there unpredictably. My tailbone often ached, my head felt squeezed at the temples, and then there was the right-upper-butt pain that never seemed to heal.

Mindful meditation often helped dissolve these sensations and discomforts. Eugene Gendlin's Focusing technique was remarkably effective also, but both methods took time and when I wanted to sleep, I wanted to sleep—not meditate or focus.

I came across a book called *The Tapping Solution* by Nick Ortner. (The tapping solution is also known as Emotional Freedom Techniques or EFT.) Theoretically, EFT can rid a person of just about any unpleasant condition.

Here is my interpretation of what's involved in a simple tapping solution exercise. (I am oversimplifying and encourage anyone interested to read the referenced book or research this online. There are YouTube videos of people doing EFT.)

First, very lightly "karate chop" the side of your hand (halfway between the pinky and wrist) while saying three times, "Even though I feel..." (fill in whatever pain or discomfort you are feeling, whether emotional or physical), "I deeply and completely accept myself."

For example, I might say, "Even though I feel intense pain in my tailbone, I deeply and completely accept myself."

Then I begin a round of tapping. Each time I tap the locations listed below, I repeat the specific pain that's bothering me. For this example, I'd tap, tap, tap, saying, "This tailbone pain, this tailbone pain, this tailbone pain" each time I'd tap the following areas.

1. Eyebrow
2. Side of eye
3. Under eye
4. Under nose
5. Mid-chin
6. Collarbone
7. Under arm
8. Top of head

You are advised to stop and assess your level of stress, pain or discomfort after each round of tapping. If it hasn't changed, repeat the cycle from start to finish. Continue as many times as desired for relief. You do not have to tap hard. It doesn't matter which side you tap. The reason the pain disappears is because we're tapping the endpoints of the meridians of energy which run down the body. Tapping theoretically unblocks these channels of energy. It's the same principle behind acupuncture.

I was surprised to find tapping dissipated my physical discomfort quite often when trying to fall asleep. Not every time, but often enough that I generally try it.

The book says that tapping halts the fight-or-flight response and reprograms the brain and body by turning off the amygdala's alarm and reprogramming the hippocampus (both are associated with fear and part of the mammalian or limbic brain). Tapping on the meridian endpoints calms the body so that the amygdala recognizes you are safe. Supposedly, tapping while accessing a specific memory or aspect of trauma will eventually reprogram your survival brain so that it's no longer triggered by that particular memory or aspect. I don't know that this is true. At present, I have no intention of voluntarily returning to graphic memories of trauma and trying it out. I could see safely using metaphorical equivalents, though.

Tapping has not, thus far, gotten rid of my PTSD symptoms, but that's not to say it isn't possible. I'm sure if I regularly worked with a trained EFT professional, which at present I can't afford, or practiced it every day on my own or tried more of the book's variations, it would help me more. But for now, I use it to get rid of my physical discomforts when I lay me down to sleep.

Again, allow me to recommend reading *The Tapping Solution*. It's well-written, well-researched, and includes many inspiring case studies.

Sorry Seems to Be the Hardest Word: Does an Apology Make Any Difference?

In a situation of abuse, especially when it is denied during and after the trauma, it's a fantastic thing to get an apology from the abuser and/or to have it recognized as having happened by those who looked the other way or initially denied the reality.

My dad was in rehab for a month in the spring of 1970. Those were the only happy days I knew between 1965 and 1970. The house we lived in no longer felt dark, cramped and small. Now, suddenly the space felt elegant, expansive and filled with light. For the first time in years, I lived without fear and it was wonderful. When I'd get home from school, I'd blast The Supremes "Farewell" album and dance around my room—happy, happy, happy.

I'd survived and now everything was going to be okay. More than okay, everything was going to be great! I'd graduate from eighth grade soon, a long glorious summer lay ahead and beyond it—a fantastic new life in high school. And when my dad came home, he'd be like he was when I was very little—kind, loving, funny, smart, thoughtful, charismatic—simply wonderful. I'd never stopped loving him. It was so obvious to me, in those rare moments I dared look in his eyes during the bad years, that something "other" had taken his place.

But now that was over. I'd see the dad I knew and loved when I looked into his beautiful blue eyes.

It was a sunny, warm afternoon the day he came home from rehab. I was the only one there. My mother was at work, my brother at school. I was lying in the sun on the patio when I heard noise through the open kitchen windows. I knew it was my dad. Instantly, my stomach clutched in cold fear, but I reminded myself he no longer drank, and without the "demon rum" in him, he would be his old self again—the one who loved me and protected me from harm, the one who would never hurt me.

I went into the house and welcomed him, giving him a big hug. He seemed preoccupied and immediately went to unpack his suitcase. I puttered around the kitchen, unsure of what to do with myself. After a while, he came out to where I was by the sink and spoke to me briefly. I won't go into what he said exactly. Words are inadequate to describe the anguish I felt in realizing that, although he was now sober, his attitude towards me hadn't changed. He still unaccountably saw me as something evil, an idea that took root in his alcoholism and remained despite his sobriety.

The dad I remembered from long ago had not come back and never would.

I did speak up about his mistreatment of me once about ten years later—not about his insane behavior from 1965-1970, but about his constant putdowns and scapegoating of me in the years that followed. My brother and I were on vacation with him in Banff, Canada after my mother died. We were staying in a gorgeous castle-like hotel on Lake Louise. Though I longed to soak up the gorgeous scenery and enjoy myself on this luxury vacation, the tension I felt and the pain in my stomach kept me from relaxing.

It was a comparatively little thing that set me off. I guess it was just one put-down too many and BAM! I was in a state of rage. I screamed and screamed and screamed at him—all the anger and resentment pouring out of me like a poison. I was out of control. As

I yelled myself hoarse, I saw the blood drain from his face. When I stopped screaming, he didn't say a word. I went back to Chicago the next day while my father and brother continued on.

My dad was never comfortable with me again for the thirty more years he lived.

I apologized several times for that outburst in the years to come and tried to talk about it with him so we could have closure and move on. But he was old-school macho. He never could talk about personal stuff like that. The truth is, everything I said to him needed to be said. It was important I stand up for myself, express my anger, tell him it was not okay to put me down and I wouldn't allow it anymore. But the way I went about it left something to be desired.

One good thing came out of it though. He didn't put me down much after that.

I often thought he and I would have had such a different life if he'd only come back from rehab and apologized.

But even if he had and we spent the rest of our lives in a wonderful father/daughter relationship (and he really did the best he could to be a great dad to me later on), it would have made no difference in terms of my PTSD symptoms because PTSD is in the body. It's a physiological response to trauma and must be healed physiologically.

It's kind of like someone breaking your legs. Their apology may be gratifying, but it won't heal your legs.

So too, an apology won't heal your PTSD, but it would be a balm upon your soul.

Who Can I Turn To:
My Visit to the Energy Healer

About a year into life without meds, the lower-stomach pain I'd had on occasion become much more frequent and severe.

GI-tract issues are common to PTSD, which makes sense since the stomach can't digest during states of fight, flight, freeze or collapse and people with PTSD are often in one of those states. Then all that's possible is constipation or diarrhea. I used to have stomach pain in the days before evacuation, (I have IBS-C), but that was it. Now there was new pain I couldn't connect to my irregularity schedule.

Just for the record, exercising regularly, eating plenty of fiber and drinking sixty-four ounces of water a day was never enough to heal my IBS-C. In my opinion, I'd had PTSD too long. My stomach just didn't know how to digest normally anymore.

When I went through that period of crying copiously for weeks and losing all the pain in my feet, I noticed something strange. Every day that I sobbed like a baby, I was "regular ". I was shocked.

If I could have, I would have cried me a river every day because nothing beats the feeling of lightness and energy I get when I'm regular. But after those initial months of daily weeping, I couldn't squeeze out more than a couple tears a day, unless inspired.

This new near-constant stomach pain was becoming intolerable. It was evenly dispersed through my lower-stomach region. It often woke me up if I fell asleep or kept me from falling asleep. There was nothing I could do to get rid of it. Not for long anyway.

Baking soda and water didn't help, nor did apple-cider vinegar, fasting or dietary changes. Mindful meditation didn't break it up. The tapping solution sometimes helped, but only briefly. The doctor I went to found no organic condition to explain my pain and, in fact, suggested I was making it up. What an (insert expletive of choice to describe the doctor here.)

I didn't know what to do.

One night, unable to sleep, I watched a fascinating PBS documentary on energy healers. They each had a different method. One healer's hands secreted a healing oil. Another healer's hands grew hot when he healed people. Another healer could see illness in the patient's energy field, grab it, and get rid of it by throwing it into a bucket of salt water. One way or another, these healers cleared the patients' energy blocks.

Inspired, I immediately searched the Internet and found an energy healer located not too far away from where I lived. Like the shaman, she had decades of experience in healing. An hour and a half session would set me back $120. I made an appointment.

It was a beautiful, cold November afternoon the day I set out for Old Town. I was cozy in jeans, sweatshirt, boots and my oversized, secondhand parka. I walked along Lake Shore Drive and west through the Gold Coast, listening to The Jonathan Simon Trio on my iPod, enjoying the invigorating lake breeze and the smell of autumn leaves. I felt optimistic.

Ann, the healer, was about sixty—a spritely figure, slim and energetic. Although the three-story walk-up she worked in was old and worn, her space was clean and bright and filled with light energy. Her beautiful oil paintings of landscapes and flowers hung throughout.

We sat across from each other beside the ancient fireplace and talked for a while. She was thorough in her intake, which lasted about half an hour. When I told her about seeing my heart as a beat-up football with old bandages hanging off it, she said it was important I visually bathe, re-bandage and heal the heart with light and love regularly.

I laid down on her padded, massage table under a light blanket with a pillow beneath my head. Ann sat immediately behind me. She said I could talk if I wanted, but I really didn't feel like it. I wanted to clear my mind, meditate and open myself up to a healing experience. Plus, I didn't want to distract her.

Not being a shaman, she didn't do any rattling, singing or dancing to start the session. Whatever guides she called in, she called in silently. They would advise her of the areas in which I needed healing and assist in sending healing energy through.

At first, when she tried tuning into me, she said there was a block over my heart and she couldn't access it. I visualized my heart bathed in light and sang a meaningful song to it in my head, feeling compassion for its wounds. Almost immediately, Ann said she was in.

Before I left for the appointment that day, I'd asked the spirit of my grandmother to come with me and assist the healer as needed. I became very relaxed as I lay there and, at one point, tangibly felt my grandmother beside me on my right. I continued to sing inside, focusing on my heart, visualizing healing light and beautiful scenarios.

Before I knew it, my session was over. Ann and I talked briefly afterwards, and then I left, walking home in a contented, dreamy state.

Back at the apartment, when I was telling Jack about my experience, I felt an unusual sensation. My face hurt like it did when I was a kid and came inside after being out in the cold too long. It was that painful thawing transition between freezing and warmth. Though that November day had been cold, it wasn't freezing—just invigorating. The pain of my facial "thaw" lasted until late the next day. I instinctively felt this was a positive thing, as well as an apt metaphor. I was coming out of the PTSD freeze state. Or at least my face was.

I also didn't have any stomach pain in the days after.

I thought this was great. Maybe the energy healer could heal my PTSD.

I went to her again the next week. This time when I came home, it was my hands that had the thawing sensation. It took from Friday to Sunday for them to feel normal again.

When I went back to the energy healer next, I took a different route. I walked down State Street and found myself before one of the bars I used to go to during my seventeenth summer. It was called The Hangge-Uppe and brought to mind an old friend named Chris. He was my brother's best friend in high school. Though I was four years younger, which was a big deal when I was thirteen, I'd always had a huge crush on him. He was handsome, absolutely brilliant, funny, creative, and he liked me a lot. That summer I graduated high school, he frequently came downtown to go dancing with me, my brother and my friends. He got married in his thirties, and then I didn't see him much at all. He died in his forties.

I took a photo of the bar and texted it to my brother with a note about how much I missed Chris.

Then I continued on to my appointment.

When I came home after another wonderful session, I felt strange. I couldn't put my finger on it. It wasn't the thawing sensation this time. It was something else, something unsettling, something I couldn't put a name to.

I told Jack about Chris. I remembered the first day I met him. I was in sixth grade and sitting in our living room, looking out the picture window. The trees had grown too still and the air was yellow-green. A tremendous summer storm was about to hit. Chris stood in the living room and introduced himself. He seemed so debonair, so worldly, so confident and sophisticated—like James Bond! When he talked to me, he really focused—as if I were the most important person in the whole world. I always felt so special when I was with Chris.

Suddenly, as I stood talking to Jack, I began to cry. How I missed Chris! I never cried when he died or in the years that followed.

I'd been in the big freeze back then, feeling so very little in states of dissociation. When I heard he died, I felt sad, but I didn't cry. I just kept pushing through the days the way I had for so many years—working a crazy, hectic schedule during the week, then sleeping it off on the weekends with lots of drugs.

Now, in my fifties, it was as if Chris had just died. I spent all weekend crying. I talked to him in my head, told him how I felt, what he'd meant to me and how sorry I was I couldn't have been more honest with him long ago when he tried to initiate a relationship in our twenties. If I'd known what was wrong with me then, things might have been different in so many ways.

Ann was definitely the real thing. Unfortunately, I didn't have the money to keep seeing her. Until such time as I did, I had to find other less expensive ways of healing.

Music, Music, Music

My father owned a bar with a jukebox. When the jukebox guy changed the records, he left behind those he removed and my dad brought them home. I remember when I was five playing these forty-fives on my little yellow record-player. I danced and sang, belting out songs like "Papa Loves Mambo", "Tell Laura I Love Her" and "Hot Diggity (Dog Diggity Boom!)". I waltzed around my bedroom to the instrumental version of "Canadian Sunset", and torch-sang "Music, Maestro, Please" in front of the mirror.

Music filled me with feelings. Wonderful feelings. All kinds of feelings: sadness, joy, melancholy, laughter, longing....

My cousins lived in two full-floor apartments below ours. One day, my oldest cousin let me borrow her little, white, square transistor radio. I laid on my bed listening to top-forty songs like "Be My Baby", "Surfer Girl", and "Sukiaki". I thought I'd die of ecstasy.

In second grade, I briefly dabbled in show business, winning First Prize with my brother at our grade school talent show. We performed songs from that year's Christy Minstrels' album, periodically turning to smile at each other as our mother advised. I hear the roar of applause still.

When we moved away and the trauma years began, music was my lifeline. Only when I listened to music did I slip out of hyperarousal or dissociation and into feelings, a whole world of feelings—raw, complex or nuanced. Music brought a kind of freedom and I loved it. The feelings were liberating, comforting, a blessing. I always felt stronger after I listened to an evocative song. For a brief moment in time, I was one with reality. No denial. I felt my feelings and trusted them. Those rare times I'd gather together enough money to buy a great forty-five, I'd play it over and over and over.

I wasn't thrilled with contemporary music in high school. 1970-1974 AM radio offered a lot of one-hit wonders and bubble-gum. I didn't connect with much of it.

"Layla" was an exception. I loved that song—the violence of emotion in the first half and the resigned sadness in the second.

I think one reason I loved the gentle opening of America's "Ventura Highway" was because my life felt so violent and unsafe. The songs on America's "Homecoming" album felt kind. My boyfriend used to play it on his eight-track tape when he drove us to Kenosha every weekend. (You could drink legally there if you were eighteen then, so it was easier for us to "pass".) My trauma era had basically been over for a couple years (or at least now I was big enough to fight or leave as needed, plus I had supportive friends), but PTSD symptoms were kicking in now—not that I knew that that's what they were. I was an insomniac and hypervigilant. If I didn't drink myself to sleep, I was awake until dawn.

I loved Tony Bennett. His music was beautiful, contemplative and dreamy. I played his albums every day after school junior and senior year. He evoked an alternate reality for me, a beautiful world filled with romance and tenderness and hope and love. I knew I'd be happy there in that world. I knew it must exist or he couldn't sing about it. No matter what I went through, it was easier to hold on if I listened to Tony. He articulated all that I didn't know I felt and couldn't name or define. I was completely, unutterably in love with the idea of him.

(I had the pleasure of actually meeting him when I was twenty-four. My girlfriend dated his bass player who introduced me to Tony in his dressing room back stage after a show. Tony was so friendly and kind and accessible, but I was so freaked out to finally meet this incredible singer who'd been so meaningful to me when I was a teenager that I literally could barely speak. After we were introduced, I shook his hand and of all the brilliant or simply complimentary things I could have said, what came out of my mouth was, "I love you". Then I slowly backed out of the room in a state of complete overwhelm. Ach!! By the way, I highly recommend his memoir *The Good Life*. It's well-written, fascinating, engaging and all-around wonderful. He is one cool guy.)

In the decades that followed, I felt mostly numb, despairing and gray.

The rare infatuation briefly pulled me into a world of color and feeling, but infatuations, by their nature, are brief.

Recreational drugs gave me a synthetic sense of wellbeing for a little while, but they were a short-term and dubious solution.

With music, I felt feelings easily and safely, and when I felt feelings, I was no longer numb and that broke up the despair. Music got into the darkness when nothing else could and turned on the light.

Splish, Splash: How to Clean Your Aura

When I was forty-nine, I burned out. I wrote about this at length in my short-read entitled *Startle: A True Story of PTSD and the Paranormal* (included in this book after the "About the Author" section.) The gist of the piece is that after a year of severe sleep deprivation (when my meds began losing their effectiveness), I started seeing things in my apartment—horrifying things. Whether I was hallucinating and/or lived in a haunted apartment and/or was in the first phase of a demonic infestation, the experience was terrifying.

After I moved out, I woke up one day suddenly able to see auras around people. (I also developed other paranormal abilities, albeit limited.)

The mediums I've come across say that people who've experienced trauma, particularly children, are more likely to have psychic abilities than those who haven't, which makes sense. Your senses naturally become keen when you go through an extended period of trauma, particularly in childhood.

As I've mentioned frequently, I went through life mostly numb and cut off from sensations and feelings.

When the meds stopped working, I began having paranormal experiences. I don't wish to alienate you, Dear Reader, so I won't go into much of that here. I bring it up for a moment in case you, too, see, smell, hear, or feel things that other people don't. Just because we live in a world of scientific materialism doesn't mean it's the only way to interpret and judge reality. I say—listen to the consensus, but in the end—trust your intelligence, your instincts, and your senses.

Anyone can learn to see auras, which are luminous energy fields surrounding people, places and things. Michael Crichton explained how he learned to see them in his fascinating memoir *Travels*. You can also research it online. I see them quickest and clearest when my eyes are tired. All I do is I stare at someone in an unfocused way. When I say unfocused, I mean I have the kind of look people get when you can tell they've temporarily stopped listening to what you're saying and are thinking about something else. I stare in this unfocused manner and the aura emerges. I haven't learned to do anything with this ability. It's mostly just fun to see at this point, although it did come in handy once when I felt sick as a dog and had no idea why until I saw a fuzzy black ball in my aura near my left kidney. I went to the doctor the next day. It turned out I had a kidney infection. I wish I knew how to remove these things. If I did, I'd walk around the hospital a block away from our apartment and casually scoop up black fuzzies from people's energy fields as I passed them.

The shamans say all illnesses show up in our energy fields before our bodies manifest them. Theoretically, then, it's a good idea to keep our auras clear, clean and vibrant.

Donna Eden wrote a wonderful book called *Energy Medicine*, chockful of quick fixes for tension, fight-or-flight states, migraines, and so on. She also talks about auras. She said taking a bath with eight ounces of baking soda cleans your aura.

For me, a bath with 12 ounces of sea salt works. It also pulls out toxins. A ten-minute soak is sufficient, although there are those who advise twenty minutes.

I've also found burning a sage smudge stick does wonders for my energy. I buy them online or at the grocery story. I light the stick and roll it through my aura from toe to head—front, back and sides.

On a related note, shaman Alberto Villoldo explains how to clean chakras in his book *Shaman, Healer, Sage (How to Heal Yourself and*

Others with the Energy Medicine of the Americas). It's best to read him in the original. I've listed those of his books I've enjoyed in my "Recommended Books" chapter. But the gist of it is: when showering, take your finger and move it in a circle a bit above your first chakra three times counterclockwise to open it up. (Imagine your body is the face of a clock to figure clockwise direction.) Pull out any dense matter you feel and throw it in the water going down the drain. Rinse your fingers. Go on to the second chakra. Repeat for all chakras. To close them, twirl your finger clockwise at each chakra location. I think this is a nice practice but I can't stand being in the shower longer than I have to. I have no idea why, but I go into hyperarousal if I'm in there too long.

Although compassionate and open to the experience of others all my life, I was rigidly closed-minded in other ways. I never believed for a moment in the paranormal or considered any New Age ideas. Once I opened my mind and began determining reality based on my experience, amazing things started happening.

When I applied the techniques detailed in Eugene Gendlin's book *Focusing*, not only did I recover lost time and body memories (some were metaphorical, but no less true), I also had flashbacks to previous incarnations. Jack and I were university students in Padua, Italy in the late 1700's. I was a guy then and Jack's roommate. I believed there was something demonic in the house we shared. He was the big-man-on-campus type and laughed it off, but I was terrified. Jack came into my world in this life when I was burned-out and seeing images in my apartment that appeared to be demonic. This time, not only did Jack not blow me off, he refused to leave my side until I felt safe.

I also spontaneously regressed to a previous life in Paris during WWII. I remembered watching the Nazis rolling in. Shudder.

My world was so very small for so many years. So very small. Work, drugs, sleep. Work, drugs, sleep. Sometimes it felt like I was buried alive. That gives me a shudder, too.

What's Going On?
Trauma Releasing Exercises

Jack is a pilot. He loves flying. He didn't receive his ticket (pilot's license) until he was in his early-sixties because he didn't have the time. He worked two jobs all his life to support his wife and six children. When I met him, he was widowed and retired.

One gorgeous summer afternoon, he was out flying alone. He'd flown out of Lansing, Illinois to Peoria and was on his way back when suddenly there appeared a small plane headed straight for him. It appeared to be stationary, not moving at all. He was taught that were he ever to find himself in such a scenario, he was to take action immediately or he'd only have seconds to live.

At first, my husband went into denial. It wasn't happening.

Then, as if waking from a dream, something inside him yelled, "Do something!"

He turned his plane sharply to the right and down, out of the killing trajectory. Seconds later, he watched the other plane fly into the space he'd evacuated. He could see the pilot looking straight ahead, still as a statue, almost as if he were frozen.

As soon as Jack landed, he noticed his hands were shaking. It only lasted a couple minutes. Then he felt normal again, calm, and grateful to have survived.

He couldn't understand why his hands shook. I told him he'd faced a threat to his survival. His body mobilized a vast energy to deal with the possibility of imminent annihilation. When he was safe again, his body released the stress hormones that had flooded his system. He discharged the trauma energy naturally, like animals in the wild do after escaping near death.

I said, "When I was little, my body was flooded with stress hormones almost every day for four years. When I felt safe again, my system, for various reasons, was unable to naturally discharge or shake out the trauma energy. In the years that followed, my body/mind tried to stabilize that energy until such time as I could release it and it ended up developing into PTSD symptoms."

It's not so easy to release trauma energy years later. When it does happen, it usually happens slowly, in bits and pieces.

I felt I'd made good progress since coming off the meds. I spontaneously shook out trauma energy pretty regularly for a year. I lost the pain in my feet with tears. I thawed out parts of my body with the help of an energy healer. It appeared that parts of my soul returned to me. I grieved people I lost and discovered lifetimes I'd forgotten. I felt emotions more deeply. I dissociated less. I had more tools at my disposal to undermine symptoms. But my hypervigilance and insomnia were still major problems and that pain in my butt muscle would not go away. It had become so disabling that I had to stop all my workouts—walking, running, tennis, aerobics, core work, everything—except for weights.

By the second spring off meds, the butt pain was sometimes so bad, I couldn't walk. I imagined the muscle hanging by a thread and was terrified of doing anything that might inadvertently cause it to sever. I believed the intense nausea I felt was related.

But every once in a while, something strange would happen, giving me pause as to the doctor's diagnosis of chronic gluteal strain. For instance, one day I limped into the bathroom and saw a gigantic cockroach sitting on the counter. We froze, staring at each other. Heart racing, I slowly genuflected and picked up one of my loafers and, well…you know what happened next. After I cleaned up the mess, called management, and met with the building's exterminator, who happened to be in the building at the time, I realized I was moving quickly, flexibly, without pain or a limp for an hour. I wondered, could the incredible pain in my butt and overwhelming nausea be buried emotional energy? Could it be the pain I "sat on" all my life? Sadness and/or anger?

Naw!

It was too big a pain. Too localized. Too tremendous. Too debilitating.

I theorized the stress hormones I felt upon seeing that cockroach acted like anesthesia, temporarily washing away all my butt pain.

At about this time, I came across Trauma Releasing Exercises (TRE). I read some really positive reviews online, so I bought the DVD narrated by the man who created the technique, Dr. David Berceli.

Trauma Releasing Exercises relax the psoas muscle at the body's core, activating natural tremors allowing for the release of tension and trauma energy stored deep in the muscles. (The psoas is the first muscle activated in fight-or-flight. It connects to muscles in the core and legs.) The people who gave testimonials at the end of the DVD said it alleviated many of their PTSD symptoms, including one WWII veteran who said he could finally sleep again.

I was excited. I imagined doing TRE for a few weeks and finally shaking out all the trauma energy that should have been released in 1970.

When I did the exercises, which, by the way, are easy, effortless and simple, the release was not like the spontaneous somatic experiencing I'd known (with coldness in my chest and involuntary trembling.) Instead, I just felt very relaxed. Sometimes I got a kind of wonderful feeling, as if a balmy, ocean breeze moved in a wave from my feet to my shoulders.

After a couple weeks of daily practice, I did not notice any significant change in my symptoms.

Then I started to notice I felt very sad within a few hours of doing TRE. Sometimes I felt overwhelmed with old feelings of despair, abandonment, betrayal, loss, loneliness, anguish, and grief. It was extremely uncomfortable because I couldn't cry it out and get relief. I'd put on my iPod and play all my saddest songs, but the tears wouldn't come.

So I stopped doing TRE.

And then, almost overnight, my whole nervous system went haywire.

I woke each morning with waves of nausea rolling through me from head to toe, back and forth, like a ship on a rollicking ocean. My arms felt numb or literally empty, as if there were no muscle or joints or bones or anything at all inside them. Other times, energy surged down my arms, particularly my left one, like a mouse running as quickly as it could from the bicep area to my hand over and over and over. My hands felt like rubber dishwashing gloves filled with water or else they felt numb. When I didn't wake with rolling nausea, I woke in a state of terror, breathless, in full-blown hyperarousal or I woke feeling as if I were about to faint. There were unpredictable moments in the course of the day in which I'd feel myself losing consciousness and have to stop, wherever I was, and put my head between my legs. Other times, I'd falter and almost literally collapse, as if I'd been severed at my center with an invisible wire. Sciatic pain arrived, forking down the back of my left leg, stabbing me with lightening pain every time I turned, sat down, stood up or leaned in any direction. In addition to my "torn" butt muscle, I had new lower back pain and an unbearably tender tailbone. My head felt squeezed at the temples. There was a knot in the back of my neck I couldn't get rid of. It felt like someone was pushing my neck down with their thumb all the time. When I fell asleep, I'd wake every half hour with a galloping heart. When I tried to nap during the day, my heart felt like a fist pushing out of my chest. And beneath all this pain and discomfort was a sorrow so tremendous, I couldn't fathom where it came from. It felt like I'd lost everyone and everything I'd ever loved. I was in such physical agony, I was sure I was dying or had an incurable disease.

I went to an internist.

All tests came back normal.

I went to the cardiologist.

All tests came back normal.

I went to a world-renowned doctor who specialized in back problems. He said I had a pinched nerve in my back, but the physical therapy he prescribed only made it worse.

The only time I wasn't in pain now was if I stood with my weight on one leg or laid down flat with my knees up.

I was in despair.

Then someone I trusted recommended her chiropractor. I immediately made an appointment.

Oh, Happy Day: The Chiropractor

As I slowly walked to the chiropractor's office, I listened to my iPod and contemplated the bizarre sense of a parallel universe I was once again experiencing. It wasn't as extreme as the winter of '98 when I felt I could drive to the suburbs and find my sixteen-year-old-self there, alive and well. But it was intense nonetheless to sense another era side by side with the one I was living in.

I felt a great sadness and an overwhelming sense of emptiness and homesickness that belonged to my mid-twenties self. It took a while to identify the source. It proved to be the sadness I didn't allow myself to feel when, in the early eighties, a great romance had died. I didn't know what made it kick in. Maybe those two weeks of TRE popped it out of a muscle or some focusing session kicked up the energy. All I knew was I was feeling the pain I blocked decades before. My body/mind knew in its wisdom I could afford the feelings now and mindfully grieve. I purposely played music from that time period, especially Joe Jackson and Phil Collins, hoping that by embracing the feelings, I'd process them quicker.

It was hot and sunny that afternoon. I walked with absurdly good posture as I imagined a ballerina would, focusing on staying centered and balanced to ward off unnecessary lower back, neck or sciatic pain. When I checked into the chiropractor's office, I couldn't sit down. Just like at home, it was too painful to put any weight on my bum.

Dr. Dan was about my age, slim, dark-haired, athletic-looking and friendly. He listened well. After taking x-rays and asking lots of questions, he said a pinched nerve in my neck would also account for my lower-back pain. He had me lay on a low-to-the-ground padded bench and pressed a finger gently into the side of my neck. Instantly, the thumb-pushing-down-my-neck feeling was gone.

Next, he tested my muscles. He had me lift my right arm parallel to the floor and asked that I resist the pressure he'd put on it. I couldn't! I was shocked. I could resist him with my left arm, but not the right. A mystery.

He did these and other things to determine where the imbalances were in my body and then corrected them with moves so obscure, I felt like he was some kind of benevolent urban witchdoctor. At the end of my appointment, he checked to see if his corrections were successful by retesting the strength of my arm. Now I could easily withstand the pressure. I felt so much better when I left that I signed up for a block of sessions.

I was tired when I got home. I laid down in the bedroom, looking forward to a nap. Just as I was about to fall asleep, the most incredible pain opened up in my solar plexus and mushroomed upwards like a poisonous cloud filling my chest. It was the meanest physical pain I'd ever known. It felt cruel.

When I got over the breathtaking shock of it, I did some deep pranic breathing—inhaling big and slow into my stomach for a count of seven, holding seven, exhaling seven, holding seven. Repeat. Tears streamed down my face. Slowly, the pain left.

I went to Dr. Dan's a couple times a week all summer and into the fall. He advised I go back to Trauma Releasing Exercises. He also taught me a few Foundational Movement Practices called Walking Pose, Seated Procedure, and Dynamic Tension.

He commented that I held myself up by my ribs. It was as if I were always leaning forward ready to run. It didn't matter if was sitting, walking or standing—I was set for take-off. He also said my body didn't know how to relax. When he'd tweak everything, straighten it out, it didn't seem to know what to do. It held itself in readiness for action.

He taught me all kinds of things—about posture, how to sit, and how to walk properly so that I wouldn't develop pain.

Slowly but surely, with each session of mild taps up the sides of my spine and gentle pressure applied to various points on my body, all the pain went away by winter and with it the morning terror, sweeping nausea, physical numbness, surging energy and vibrations, and feelings of imminent collapse and unconsciousness.

I never thought to tell Dr. Dan about the mean solar plexus pain that came when I laid down after every session with him. I'd just forget to mention it. I think the pain came only after I saw him because he always straightened out my body from the protective and defensive postures I assumed as a child and in so doing, unloosed buried emotional energy. The solar plexus pain stopped coming when I stopped seeing him.

Hello, Goodbye:
Leaving the Freeze State

In *Waking the Tiger*, Peter Levine talks about how staff in MASH units would say, in reference to soldier-patients going under anesthesia, "As they go in, so they go out". This meant that whatever state the soldiers were in before surgery—agitated, relaxed, dissociated and so on—was the state in which they'd come out of it.

When a person instinctively and involuntarily freezes in trauma (and it's always involuntary and instinctive, the survival brain doesn't think), they often dissociate and go numb. I went numb for decades. I still felt things, but almost as if I was shot up with Novocain.

After I got off the meds, I was, from time to time, flooded with overwhelming nausea. Usually I woke with it first thing, but sometimes it hit me during the day or evening. It often felt as if I were going to vomit and/or faint.

At first, I thought the nausea had to do with IBS-C. My digestive tract was so messed up from years of of fight, flight or freeze that my digestive process consisted of constipation for two or three weeks, followed by diarrhea—which temporarily screwed up my blood pressure and electrolytes.

I also thought it possible the nausea was due to the effect of the stress hormone cortisol on my stomach.

It took me almost two years to realize it was something else.

My nausea was a physical manifestation of emotion.

It wasn't anger anymore. I had a lot of that once, but got rid of most of it over the years with strenuous work-outs—aerobics, running, weights, hitting a punching bag and vigorously returning tennis balls pitched by a machine.

As time went by, I learned the overwhelming nausea was the sadness I felt as a child, with an underlayment of anguish, terror and a sense of abandonment.

I couldn't stand the feeling. It was difficult to cry now unless I was in tremendous pain. My eyes might hurt from unshed tears, my throat thicken and burn, but still the tears wouldn't come.

To my surprise, Trauma Releasing Exercises (TRE) proved to be the solution.

I'd gone back to doing them at the recommendation of the chiropractor.

Every day, I'd lie on the floor in my bedroom and ask the spirit of my deceased mother, my guardian angel, my spirit guide, my higher self and my body/mind to please help me release the sadness. Then I'd slip in my iPod earbuds and listen to a playlist of sad or evocative songs while I did TRE. I tried not to think of trauma memories or sad things for long, since that threw me back into my thinking brain and out of communication with my body and survival brain. Instead, I'd try to focus on where the sadness was lodged— usually in my stomach, ribs, lower back and tailbone.

In the beginning, it was hit or miss with the tears. Sometimes I cried, sometimes I didn't. Then, one day, a miracle happened. I found I could cry every single time I practiced TRE. What a relief! Although crying was unpleasant, afterwards I felt lighter, happier, more energetic and balanced.

And the nausea always went away.

Back when I was little, I was underweight all the time because I felt too sick to my stomach to eat.

I always felt nauseous. Now I know that feeling was sadness.

As they used to say in MASH units, "As they go in, so they go out."

Here's hoping that applies to me.

Smile: PTSD Teeth

In 1964, when I was eight, the dentist told my mother I was grinding my teeth at night. Through the decades that followed, all my dentists commented that I was grinding my teeth. What could I do? How could I stop what I did in my sleep? I was offered no remedy.

Turns out, I actually wasn't grinding them. I was clenching them. I can't tell you how many times I woke and had to pry my top teeth apart from my bottom. It was a bizarre morning ritual.

In my late forties, a dentist suggested I get a tooth guard. I'd never heard of such a device, which was unfortunate because by that time, my teeth were really starting to disintegrate. They were becoming increasingly transparent and the top front ones were chipping off in little geometric bits. The dentist said there was nothing that could be done, although a tooth guard would prevent further damage.

I found this depressing. I had beautiful teeth once and they were beginning to look kind of bad.

It came as no surprise to find that people with PTSD are significantly more likely to grind or clench their teeth (bruxism) when they sleep compared to people without PTSD. They also show higher incidences of gum disease.

I did some research online to see if there were any home remedies to strengthen weak teeth. I'd found quite a few solutions on earthclinic.com (apple cider vinegar for sinus headaches! Baking soda for ailing kidneys!), so I thought I'd see what people from around the world had to say, if anything, about thinning teeth.

There were amazing stories about the wonders of Black Walnut liquid extract (you can purchase it online in dropper bottles). The Earthclinic folks said Black Walnut re-mineralizes your teeth and builds them back up. They also said it can get rid of cavities. I had nothing to lose but ten dollars by giving it a try.

For the last three years, I've taken one dropper's worth of Black Walnut once a day, every day. (Recommended daily doses allow for more.) I also took a multivitamin with one hundred percent of recommended daily minerals and ate a super healthy diet with a lot of fruit, vegetables, salmon, and lean meat.

I happened to notice recently that my teeth aren't as transparent as they used to be. The thin parts have actually filled in enough for me to notice.

So if your teeth have suffered from clenching or grinding, you might want to give Black Walnut a try as well as consuming more minerals in your diet.

...

On a related note, did you ever have a dream where your teeth were falling out or crumbling? I had it many times. I mentioned it to my psychiatrist once. He said it is famously known to occur when you are undergoing tremendous, unsustainable stress. I mention this after watching a show where a dream interpreter told a client it meant you wanted to get pregnant.

Not!

Imagine: Intrusive Thoughts

I remember watching *Psycho* for the first time when I was thirteen. I'd heard about it in graphic detail from friends and made sure to look away at the end when they showed the skeleton. I dint want to see no skeleton.

I used to get scared pretty easily watching horror movies. My parents would say, "It's only a movie." Still, I felt safer knowing I could look away from the screen when I wanted and usually did.

Then there were decades I wouldn't bat an eye watching the most violent, horrifying movies. Those were the dissociation years.

That would be a good show. *The Dissociation Years.* Kind of like *The Wonder Years,* except it would have been one episode after another of me interacting with people and showing a total lack of affect no matter what horrific thing happened. The show would be in black and white. At the end of each episode, something incredibly horrible would happen, but I'd never change my expression. Then, in the season finale, when the very bad thing happened at the end of the show, instead of my usual non-responsive, inappropriate lack of affect, I'd widen my eyes, gasp, and color would fill the screen. The audience would go crazy.

Of course, I wasn't totally shutdown for decades. There were times I was triggered into states of out-of-control fight-or-flight behavior.

But no matter what state I was in, dissociated or in overwhelm, hypervigilance was at my core.

Off the meds, I began to feel more deeply again, which was great if I was watching cute little kittens, but not so great when it had to do with some aspect of man's inhumanity to man.

I was reading Alberto Villoldo the other night and he mentioned something I've come across before. Our survival brain doesn't know the difference between what we imagine and what we are actually seeing before us in real life.

This is great when beautiful memories come to my mind, but not so much with awful ones, because my PTSD nervous system responds to the awful ones as if they are happening in the present moment.

I have found for me, it's okay to look back, but I best not stare.

When I have intrusive thoughts, which are always unpleasant ones, it sometimes feels like I can't get them out of my head. I don't want to trigger anyone, including me, so I won't go into detail as to the nature of those I have.

For a long time, I derailed them by doing something more powerful—either physically, like working out with music blasting, or intellectually engaging, like watching a riveting documentary. Because I tended to go into hyperarousal with intrusive thoughts, my inclination has always been to take action fast rather than going within via something like mindful meditation. Even though I knew meditation would kill the thoughts dead, it was too hard for me to sit still when my heart was racing. (Not that sitting still is necessary to mindful meditation. It's just the way I do it.)

TRE is a great choice to kill intrusive thoughts and hyperarousal dead because it involves movement as well as feeling sensations within. Once my psoas muscle is relaxed, it sends a message to my survival brain that I am no longer in danger. The stress hormones stop flooding. Oxygen stops pumping to my muscles, lungs and heart. Blood pressure and pulse come down. Intrusive thoughts scatter.

There are certain times of the day and certain circumstances that almost act like fly paper in attracting repetitive, obsessive, lousy thoughts. Because it has become so predictable, I have a greater sense of the illusory aspect of whatever thought has kicked in and it has become a teensy bit easier to step back and detach.

In the olden days, I'd get drunk or take massive amounts of drugs to obliterate whatever was in my head. I don't blame myself for doing that. It was the best solution I could come up with at the time. But now, thank goodness, I have other options.

Both Sides Now:
Another Look at Nausea

I was so excited to see *Nausea* by Jean-Paul Sartre on the reading list in a class I took in college. I'd been feeling various degrees of nausea almost constantly since I was nine and hoped I would find some kind of epiphanic answer in this famous existential novel to finally explain it and pull me out of the mysterious dissociated, robotic state I was in at university while everyone around me seemed to be having the time of their lives.

I vividly remember sitting on the vinyl couch in my apartment, smoking cigarettes and drinking hot chocolate as I read *Nausea*. When I finished it, I thought I must have missed something and kept rereading the final pages. The tree was bothering him? So quit looking at the tree.

I spent a good deal of my adult life feeling mildly sick to my stomach. It was usually at a low level, but enough so that I was never very hungry. When people asked how I stayed so slim, I'd say, "It's easy. I'm always nauseous."

About a year ago, I stubbed my toe so badly, it broke. I iced it on and off for hours, took ibuprofen and was able to fall asleep around three a.m. I woke at five with throbbing pain in my foot and nausea so overwhelming, I felt like I could drown in it.

It didn't respond to baking soda and water or any of the ordinary GI-related remedies. It seemed to be in an untouchable class all its own. It did go away after a couple hours, but I wondered—how could

I get such incredible nausea from an injury?

A few days later, I did some research.

When your body/mind perceives it is injured, your system initiates the fight-or-flight response, shunting your blood to those areas immediately needed for fighting or running, and away from the organs you don't need at that moment, like the stomach. This can cause nausea and vomiting.

Not long after I read that, I laid down for a nap.

Suddenly, nausea pushed up inside like a toxic spill. I felt so sick, I could barely breathe.

I thought, *If my body has perceived a threat from injury precipitating the shunting of my blood away from my stomach, it is clearly capable of nuanced perception. What if I treat my body as if it is a separate entity from me? What if I try to calm it down with a physical gesture like I would to someone I loved?*

Instinctively, as if I were comforting a dear friend, I slowly, gently, smoothed my right palm over my left forearm over and over for a few minutes, saying softly, "There, there. Everything is alright now. There, there." I focused on the felt-sense of that comforting, soothing sensation.

The nausea went away completely! I was thrilled.

Previously, I realized that I become overwhelmed with nausea when flooded with sadness. This might suggest that my body perceives overwhelming sadness and the attendant cortisol as much as a threat as it does physical injury. I'm not sure, though, which comes first. Cortisol or sadness.

In any event, it is a great thing to know that if I make an effort to communicate with my survival brain, it will listen and respond.

Do It Again: Somatic Therapy

After reading several books by Alberto Villoldo, I was in love with the idea of finding a true shaman to help me heal. I tried without success finding someone local who'd been trained by Villoldo, but I did find one in Colorado who recommended the best one he knew in the Chicagoland area. Not only was she a well-trained shaman with decades of experience, but also a licensed therapist trained in Somatic Experiencing. I made an appointment.

I could only afford a few sessions ($120/hour). For two of them, she went on journeys with her spirit guides to heal me. In another, she helped me cut unhealthy energy ties to people in my life, past and present, with a meaningful ritual. She did one long-distance healing once when I was too sick to take the train to her office. In our last session, we did somatic therapy.

D. was a gentle, quiet person. I liked her and I liked her office. It was small, cozy, and peaceful. I felt safe there. Unlike the first shaman, this one took less than thirty seconds to call in her spirit guides. She shook a rattle and softly sang a brief song under her breath. No big dance or drama with this shaman.

For my Somatic Experiencing session, she closed her eyes to receive counsel from her guides and journey into my past while I sat across from her in a relaxed state.

When she opened her eyes again, she said she saw a little girl running in terror from a huge, dark, inhuman energy. She had no protection, nowhere safe to go.

Then she took a teddy bear that had been behind my chair and placed it on the floor between me and the door.

She said, "That dark energy I saw terrorizing the little girl has just walked in."

Immediately, I froze. I felt physically immobile from the waist down, but found myself leaning forward from the waist up. I kept looking from the vulnerable teddy bear on the floor to the dark entity by the door and back again. I was filled with almost unbearable energy, painfully alert, my muscles constricted. I felt paralyzed between equal parts fear and the need to grab the bear and protect him.

The shaman said, "What do you want to do?"

I said, "I want that dark thing out of here."

She said, "Move it out. You can dispose of him in whatever way you choose."

Using the immense energy circulating my system, I pushed the dark figure out the door, into the elevator, down to the first floor and onto the sidewalk. I saw a pick-up truck pull to the curb and two men jump out to load the hulk into the back. Then they got back into the truck and drove off. It was done.

I felt such relief. My body relaxed. I could move again.

I did, in retrospect, feel bad for a moment that I didn't immediately pick up the bear when the dark energy came into the room. But had I sensed him make a move closer, I know I would have grabbed the bear, because as a child, I'd done as much when others I loved were in danger.

Therapists and their PTSD clients often use metaphors in healing. Talking about the details of specific traumas often serves only to nail the memories deeper into the psyche without relief. It can also retraumatize. Metaphors can recreate trauma dynamics, allowing for their safe discharge. Some people worry they cannot heal unless they remember what happened in lost time, but it isn't true. My traumatic experiences weren't healed one bit with analysis and discussion. (I have three blocks of lost time. One short. Two a month long. I don't care to know what happened. I get the gist of it—overwhelm!—and my survival brain did what it needed to do to protect me.)

There are wonderful examples of somatic therapy sessions in books like *Waking the Tiger* and *The Body Remembers* (see "Recommended Reading" at the end of this book.) Peter Levine explains renegotiating the original trauma, breaking free of the immobility response, and changing the ending of what happened by engaging the body's felt-sense.

After I got rid of that big, dark hulk, I did not discharge energy like I did in the first year off meds, with a chill in my chest and uncontrollable trembling, although I did feel mighty relaxed and happy afterwards—especially when the shaman told me that the Spirit of Bear volunteered to keep that little girl safe forever and ever. He would never leave her side.

. . .

Speaking of Spirit Animals or Power Animals, I never heard of them before I was in my fifties. When I did, it made sense of a strange experience I had in my mid-forties.

I was still taking meds, but had quit painkillers. I woke one night and got out of bed to relieve myself. When I returned, I scooted to the far end, as I always did, to push my back up against the wall. (That always made me feel safe.) The moment I lay still, I felt the spirit of an enormous bear lie down beside me. I couldn't see him, but I felt him. I was instantly infused with the greatest sense of wellbeing I had ever known in my life. Never had I felt so comforted, so safe, so loved. I fell instantly to sleep.

When I woke the next morning and remembered, I was completely baffled. I didn't know what to make of it. It wasn't a dream. Without any knowledge of non-ordinary reality, I couldn't make sense of it—but I longed for the Bear to come back.

In my early fifties, I burned-out. I lost a lot of confidence. I didn't want to see anyone. I lost my job and couldn't stand my new one. I went to work, came home and that was it. I felt so low, so down and out, that I wouldn't go anywhere if I didn't have to. I wouldn't even walk down the street. I just took cabs if I had to go somewhere. I felt like I lost my spirit.

One morning, just before waking, a beautiful black horse appeared to me in a dream. He was so vivid, so tangibly real—I can see and feel him still. He touched his nose to my forehead and I immediately woke, filled with energy, confidence and wellbeing. The horse had infused me with his spirit.

Once I found out there were such things as spirit animals and power animals, I understood who the bear and the horse were. They each gave me a gift when I needed it most.

I haven't seen either one since, but I shall never forget them.

Thank you Spirit of the Bear and Spirit of the Horse!

Tell Me Why: Did I Choose to Have PTSD for This Incarnation?

I recently read a thought-provoking book called *Soul's Plan* by Robert Schwartz. The book suggests we have all reincarnated many, many times, and before each incarnation, we choose what we will work on in the next life in order to evolve as souls and become closer to God. Mr. Schwartz gives case studies of people who, with the aid of mediums, find out why they chose such a difficult life or a life of tragedy or illness this time around.

If it is true that we voluntarily reincarnate with specific challenges, I thought I'd take a look at what issues have come up again and again as a result of having PTSD. Have I become a better person, directly or indirectly, as a result of it? What positive qualities have I developed that I may not have without it?

I learned to read before going to school. I was a quick study and smart. Things came so easily, I rarely had to apply myself. I got bored quickly and stopped finishing projects if there was no challenge to them. I remember reading the fable of the tortoise and the hare. The hare ridiculed the turtle because he was so slow. When the turtle challenged the hare to a race, the hare was so confident he'd win, that he took a nap and woke to find the tortoise had won the race. I was a little nervous when I read that story. Although I was kind and didn't ridicule people, I was afraid I would end up losing somehow because I had no need to learn perseverance.

I have certainly learned it now. Twenty-five years of traditional talk-therapy and the focused application of my intellect did not make my PTSD symptoms go away. I did not give up. I have learned perseverance.

Thanks to frequent states of hyperarousal, I have had access to tremendous amounts of energy to offer employers. I generally worked harder and longer than everyone else anywhere I worked. If there was a problem, my bosses knew I wouldn't give up until I found the solution. My PTSD energy wouldn't let me! I learned tenacity.

I have been in good shape since I was a teenager (with the exception of the period in which I took Zyprexa). With stress hormones flooding through me so much of my life, working out was one of my only outlets. At the age of 59, I am still 123 pounds at 5'-7". (I was the fastest runner in grade school. Part of that was genes. Part of that was a constant readiness to take flight!) I have excellent muscle tone and build muscle easily. This might be, in part, because the cortisol that regularly floods through me is not only a stress hormone, but also a steroid. (That's my theory anyway.)

I'm excellent in an emergency, calm as a cucumber. When my external and internal environments are in agreement, I am at peace.

I am well-read. Isolated for so many years, I had a lot of alone-time and spent most of it reading—always looking for solutions to fix what ailed me. I read countless biographies, memoirs and histories of people who survived all manner of tragedy in order to find out how they healed or came out whole.

I learned to develop patience and tolerance—especially when people denied my reality—in order not to explode and hurt others. I've tried to practice acceptance of people, places, things and situations as they are, in order to have some measure of serenity.

I've become less judgmental. When I look at the mistakes I've made, it's easier to understand how others can make them, too. I believe everyone is trying to do the best they can most of the time.

I can walk into a room and instantly assess the emotional environment because I unconsciously read people's body language—the result of my childhood when sensing moods felt necessary to survive. My senses became overdeveloped. I have excellent peripheral vision. My sense of smell is ridiculous. I did begin to lose hearing in grade school. It was genetic. I think it's noteworthy, though, that I retained high frequency hearing. It allowed me to hear "warning" sounds like garage doors going up and bottles clinking.

Children who experience trauma are more likely to become psychic than those who do not. When it became apparent the meds stopped working when I was forty-nine, I burned-out and suddenly had so many paranormal experiences, I almost went nuts. Now I smell ghosts all the time. I see and feel them, too, but less often than I smell them. When I've gone into meditative trances, trapped souls have stepped forward and told me their stories. It's a great thing to know for a fact that there is a spirit world, that this PTSD-life isn't the end.

Having known so much pain and loneliness, I have a lot of compassion. I'm always on the side of the underdog. I try to help others. I put myself in other people's shoes.

I do not deny reality as much as I once did. When my survival brain froze me as a kid, I was instantly, automatically, involuntarily removed. It was as if the emotional core of me receded inward, shrinking to an infinitesimal speck, while the external physical part of me was shot up with Novocain. Then when the crazy stuff went down around me, it didn't feel quite as real. As an adult, I denied inappropriate behavior time and time again—sometimes because my survival brain dissociated me, sometimes because I honestly just couldn't tell exactly what was happening.

I think one of the issues I might have chosen to work on in this incarnation is forgiveness. I've made progress, but there are still a couple incidents I'm not sure I've forgiven. I've forgotten them for long stretches, put them out of my head, but when the memories return, so too does the rage and resentment. Then I slip into hyperarousal and have to take action to break out of it.

I think part of the reason I haven't completely let go of these old hurts is the fear that someday, if I'm not vigilant and I don't hold these bad memories and angry feelings close, I'll dissociate in a similar scenario and bad things will happen again.

It's an illusion I can stop dissociation from happening. It's an involuntary process of the survival brain, just like breathing. I need to remember that so I don't become demoralized.

My PTSD has significantly undermined my quality of life since I was very young. It's brought great pain, sorrow, loneliness and despair, but it has also made me more loving, kind and compassionate. I've also become someone who never gives up.

If I agreed to have PTSD before I came into this life so that I'd become a more loving, compassionate soul, it worked.

Now that I've clearly fulfilled my soul's purpose…I'd like my PTSD removed!

Cry Me a River: Trauma Releasing Exercises (TRE)—One Year Later

As mentioned previously, when I first started doing TRE, I got very sad within a few hours of doing them. I did not like that. It wasn't just that sadness felt unpleasant. It was because it was physically so difficult for me to get the tears out. It had been that way for decades. I'd get signs of imminent weeping, but unless I felt unbearable physical pain, the tears usually wouldn't come. So I stopped doing TRE, until the chiropractor recommended I start them up again.

Every day, I'd close the door to my bedroom, do the TRE warm-up exercises, lie down on a blanket, slip my iPod earbuds in and start shaking out my psoas. I'd play sad songs and occasionally squeeze out a tear or two, but for a few weeks, the enterprise was almost fruitless lachrymose-wise.

I remembered back to those early days off the meds when I cried copiously and lost all the pain in my feet. I remembered how it even affected my GI tract, allowing me astonishing regularity for a little while. I slept better, too.

How I longed to find the secret to weeping!

Before each TRE session, I began asking my body/mind to release the sadness and asking any angels and spirit guides and the spirit of my mother to help me let go of the buried energy. Since the chiropractor told me I held my sadness in the center of my solar plexus, I began focusing on that area during TRE. Sometimes, when I gently felt my ribs or pressed into my stomach, I burst into tears.

Crying became easier and easier. Over the course of the last year in which I practiced TRE daily, there were times I wept three times a day. As the months passed, I didn't even need the jumpstart of TRE to cry. It came easily now.

At the risk of sounding like a broken record, I really didn't like crying and couldn't stand it sometimes, but I knew it was somehow healing my body and soul. And when I had a vivid dream in which I was told I would be healed once I filled a large bowl with my tears, I knew there was an end date to all this sadness.

Between my fifteen chiropractic sessions and daily TRE, the following pain and discomforts have either disappeared or been significantly reduced:

Sciatic pain (gone)

Gluteal pain (gone)

Tailbone pain and tenderness (This is gone for the most part. It seems to return briefly with primary-family-related stress.)

Lower back pain (gone)

Neck pain (gone)

Surging energy propelling up and down my arms (Comes back only with great stress.)

Feeling of empty or numb arms (gone)

Hands that feel like rubber gloves filled with water (gone)

Face pain, like it's made of marble (gone)

Heart beating out of my chest twenty minutes after going to sleep (Comes back with great stress.)

Nausea sweeping through my body in waves (gone)

Head squeezed at the temples (Comes and goes with stress.)

Feelings of extraordinary weakness, near-faint, and imminent physical collapse (gone)

When I watched Berceli's TRE DVD, practitioners said they slept a lot better. For me, my ability to fall asleep and stay asleep has improved, but remains elusive under stress.

I still have symptoms of IBS-C, but that also has improved. I am not completely constipated for weeks at a time. And when the constipation ends, diarrhea doesn't necessarily follow. My GI tract appears to be digesting easier.

I am still exhausted most of the time, but if I cry, the fatigue lifts and I have energy for a few hours.

I still set aside time to cry every day. I've often wondered when all the old sadness will be released. Given that I dissociated as a child, as well as consciously "blocked out" sadness and overwhelming feelings, and continued to bury them in the decades that followed, I suppose it might take longer than a year.

Spooky: Residual Hauntings and Trauma Energy

One night, I watched the psychic/medium show *The Haunting of...
with Kim Russo*. The guest star was Orlando Jones. He told his story
of checking into a hotel in North Carolina years before and almost
immediately leaving because of a paranormal experience. When Kim
returned with him, she picked up the details of a trauma that
occurred in his hotel room fifty years earlier. She said there were no
trapped spirits in the space. No ghosts had ever tried to frighten or
communicate with him. Instead, what he'd walked into was a
residual haunting, which is a sort of movie clip of an old trauma that
plays over and over on a loop until the original energy is expended
and fades to nothing.

Kim told Orlando that environments absorb trauma energy and
gave the example of Civil War battlefields that still ring with the
sound of cannon fire and the shouts of soldiers over a century later.
That reminded me of psychics who can lead police to violent crime
scenes in woody areas without being told the crime locations because
the earth, trees and air absorb the trauma energy and the psychics feel
and see it.

Many years ago, before I knew any of this, I facetiously
conjectured that the reason the home I grew up in sold so often was
because the familial energy we left behind continues to haunt the
rooms.

All this reminded me of PTSD flashbacks, body memories,

intrusive thoughts, and even my parallel universe experiences. Our bodies absorb trauma energy when we can't escape the violence (and all trauma is a kind of violence to the body and soul, even without physical contact) and can't process it due to circumstances beyond our control. Eventually it emerges to be felt and processed again and again until all the energy is discharged. It moves in cycles, as all of life does.

The show confirmed for me that the more I feel and release the emotional energy that has been locked inside, the closer I come to being free of the frozen past.

You Are Not Alone:
The Secret Life of Plants

The Secret Life of Plants by Peter Tompkins and Christopher Bird begins with the true story of a man named Cleve Backster, an interrogation specialist for the CIA, and his mind-blowing experiment. One night in the sixties, he was alone in his office. There was nothing decorative in the room, except for a plant his secretary gave him to brighten up the space. He'd been giving polygraphs all day and decided, just for the fun of it, to attach the electrodes of his lie detector to the plant. He wondered if it would have a pulse and, if so, how it might change if he burned one of its leaves. He remembered there was a book of matches in his secretary's drawer. Before he even turned to get it, the galvanometer went wild. He was astonished. It was as if the plant read his mind.

He thought it had to have been an accident.

He tried experiment after experiment and was astonished to find the plant somehow seemed to understand his thoughts and intentions.

In the years that followed, he and dozens of scientists performed countless experiments showing not just that plants are intelligent and respond to love and kindness, hatred and cruelty, but also that once a bond is formed between a plant and its caretaker, loving energy directed towards that plant had the power to heal.

It was further discovered it wasn't just plants that responded to focused loving energy. Water, human cells, all kinds of living matter responded and healed to the power of love's energy.

The implications and possibilities were mindboggling, especially the idea that people might be able to heal themselves and others by directing loving energy to diseased cells and painful conditions.

Sometimes, when I've sent love to areas of my body bunched up in pain, it has made a difference.

One night, before the days I cried away the pain in my feet, they woke me from a deep sleep. I got out of bed and went into the den. There I sat on the couch, exhausted, wondering how many hours I'd be up with the pain. My feet were burning, vibrating with pain. Instinctively, I did something I'd never done before. I picked up one stockinged foot, cradled it in my hands and massaged it compassionately, saying, "I'm sorry, little foot, I'm sorry you are in so much pain. You should never have to feel like this. Why, you're the sweetest little foot in all the universe, the dearest, most wonderful foot that ever was and I couldn't love you more."

All the pain in that foot disappeared. I assumed it was because I'd given it a nice massage and it would come back in a moment. I picked up the other foot, massaged it the same way, and said the same loving words with the same compassionate feeling.

The pain in that foot disappeared also.

I sat back on the couch, so happy to be without pain for however many minutes it lasted. When the pain didn't come back after twenty minutes, I went to bed and slept. Now I wonder if my feet responded to loving kindness.

...

Ever since I read *The Secret Life of Plants,* I'm convinced prayer, or directed loving energy, can make a difference so whenever I see anyone download this book, I say a prayer for them. I figure it can't hurt and it only takes a moment. Maybe pain is part of the human condition and necessary for our development as evolving souls, but that doesn't mean I won't do what I can to alleviate it.

Hurts So Bad: When Stomach Pain Wakes You in the Night

When I stopped going to the chiropractor (due to a lack of funds), I stopped getting that tremendous stomach pain which followed every appointment. Though it never lasted long, it had been awful and I was glad to be rid of it.

I felt optimistic. So much of my physical pain had gone. Everything seemed to be improving.

Then one day, apropos of nothing I recall, the billowing solar plexus pain returned. It began waking me from a sound sleep several nights a week, sometimes several times in a single night. It was still as mean as ever. Once I was completely alert, it faded.

It was bizarre. It was almost as if I were being sent a message, but from who? And what did they want? I couldn't decipher the code.

It wasn't acid indigestion. I drank an anti-inflammatory drink every day (three tbs. apple cider vinegar, juice of one lemon, two tsp. maple syrup, eight oz. water). I checked my pH daily with pH strips from the pharmacy. It was always a healthy 7.25 to 7.35.

My GI tract was considerably better. Plus, this pain wasn't anything like that old pre-diarrhea pain, which was located a lot lower down.

Knowing I spent a lifetime flooded with cortisol, it occurred to me that that might be what was causing me tummy trouble. I did some research and learned the following.

Symptoms of High Levels of Cortisol:
Nausea, heartburn, abdominal cramps, diarrhea or constipation
Insomnia
Fatigue
Weight gain, especially around abdomen even though you eat well and exercise
Lowered immunity to infections
Craving high glucose foods
Backaches and headaches
Low sex drive
Anxiety
Depression

Foods/Substances that Increase Cortisol:
Mr. Booze
Caffeine
Cigarettes
Refined sugar
Junk Food
Fruit Juice
Carbs without fiber (bread, cereal, cookies, crackers)
Fat-free and low-fat yogurt (High quality yogurt containing probiotic bacteria is good.)
Over-processed vegetable and seed oil (canola, corn, soy and sunflower oil)
Factory-farmed beef (Grass-fed beef is fine.)

Things that Lower Cortisol
Nutrient-dense food
Fish Oil (Research shows 2000 mgs. a day will lower cortisol, but I couldn't find how much it took to reach therapeutic levels.)

Rhodiola

Holy Basil Extract

Mindful meditation

Running slower! (An article in *HuffPost* said strenuous running raises cortisol whereas relaxed jogging or less aggressive heart-rate exercises don't. They didn't explain why. Maybe it's because in some people the survival brain interprets running and the attendant rise in blood pressure as indicative of threat, so it keeps activating the release of stress hormones. They say if you do run, taking a Vitamin C afterwards buffers the rise of cortisol. In *Waking the Tiger,* Peter Levine wrote that Viet Nam vets with PTSD and a group of people without PTSD were all given a medication which slightly raised their blood pressure. The people without PTSD did not notice much of any change whereas the PTSD vets went into flashbacks. For some people, raised blood pressure triggers.)

Based on my theory that too high a level of cortisol was causing me stomach pain, I added Rhodiola, Holy Basil Extract and Fish Oil Supplements to my daily regimen. I began eating salmon a couple times a week. I reduced my Coca Cola intake to one can a day and went from ten cigarettes a day to five.

For a few weeks, I didn't wake with stomach pain. I was delighted! I figured my lowered cortisol intake did the trick.

Until the pain came back.

I couldn't figure it out. And why did it only come at night after I fell asleep?

I did more research. This time, I discovered my symptoms fit the diagnosis of a duodenal ulcer.

Ugh.

I got the name of a gastroenterologist and made an appointment. An endoscopy couldn't be scheduled for a month, but she gave me meds in the meantime. They didn't help at all. I white-knuckled through the pain in the weeks before the procedure. At the last minute, I realized this doctor wasn't covered by my insurance, so I had to cancel. I found another gastroenterologist who came highly recommended, but he wouldn't be able to see me for eight weeks.

All I could do was hold on.

Gonna Take a Miracle:
All the Pain I Never Felt

I was on my way back to the energy healer.

One reason I hadn't gone back to her was because I just didn't have the extra money. I didn't really have it now either, but I was desperate. My solar plexus pain was indescribable. I could barely breathe when it hit and now it hit often. My endoscopy was scheduled for October. I hoped the doctor could diagnose what ailed me and fix it.

In the meantime, I needed help and I needed it fast.

My beloved ninety-eight year old uncle (Roy), who lived alone in Arizona, was in trouble and I needed to get out there. His health had deteriorated suddenly. He was in a lot of pain from various conditions and could no longer make his own meals or drive. He got around the house with difficulty, bent over a rolling cart. His latest setback was a urinary blockage requiring a catheter. A cystoscopy had been scheduled, but it wasn't for two weeks. His catheter kept migrating and 9-1-1 had been called several times. The EMTs and fire fighters repeatedly told my dear cousin, who lived in Roy's gated community, our uncle needed to be in an assisted-living facility or nursing home. But Roy had free will and a clear, brilliant mind. No one could force him to do what he didn't want to, and he'd made it clear for years he intended to die in his home.

He'd worked like a dog all his life to buy a beautiful home on the golf course. He'd gone without, carefully saving and investing, while taking care of my grandmother until she died. He got married for the first time in his seventies only to have his wife develop Alzheimer's within two years. He took care of her in their home, with professional help, until her death eight years later.

He'd always taken loving care of other people. Now he needed help. But I would be of little use with the stomach pain that brought me to my knees every day. This was one instance in which weeping had done nothing to dissolve my pain.

I also needed to get my license quickly, so I could drive my uncle wherever he needed to go or to run errands. Since I hadn't driven since 1980, I'd have to take a driving test for the first time since I was sixteen (1973).

So there I was with only a few days to get my license (my permit would expire within the week), find a way to alleviate my stomach pain and fly to Arizona.

It was still warm in Chicago. In spite of my pain, I enjoyed the walk from our apartment in Streeterville to Old Town. It took me through the neighborhoods I'd lived in since I moved downtown with my parents in 1974.

There was Pearson Street, just behind Water Tower Place, where I lived in my late thirties and early forties, working sixty hours a week at a high-pressure, deadline-driven job. It was also where I became addicted to painkillers, buying two hundred a week from the doorman.

Then came Walton Street where I worked in a little bookstore in my early twenties after my mother died, feeling numb, not caring if I lived or died, and glad not to care.

I cut through the historic Drake Hotel, where I spent many hours in the perennial twilight of the Coq D'Or Bar under the stairs.

I walked down Oak Street next, where I took cigarette breaks when I managed the biggest realty company in Chicago.

On to Rush Street, where I briefly lead a lush life in my teen years. I still remember the terrifying hangovers of flooding adrenalin, racing heart and fear, fear, fear as if it were yesterday.

Walking past Goethe Street, I looked east and saw the corner buildings at Astor Street and Ritchie Court where I lived in my teens and twenties. Back then, I felt so empty inside, as if some core part of me had withdrawn or died. How it baffled me. Nor could I understand those occasions, rare as they were, when I'd completely lose it—scream my voice hoarse, break up with boyfriends, quit jobs, write crazy letters to people I hadn't talked to in years, mailing them at three in the morning.

Finally, I came to Wells Street, where I lived in a $295 a month walk-up while managing a bookstore in my late twenties. I had some good times there until they renovated the 1885-structure and cockroaches infested my apartment.

I stopped down the street at the home of my old pal, Al. I'd had little continuity in my life—socially speaking. There'd been so many friends I'd made and lost because people just couldn't count on me as a rule. I'd be fine for a little while at the beginning, consistent in personality, dependable, and good company. And then suddenly, I'd drop out, become unavailable, unplug from the world, change phone numbers and addresses. I'd feel so dead inside I couldn't bear it, couldn't bear to be with anyone, have anyone see me that way. I wanted to disappear so often, exist less, sleep the pain away. The few times I did try to explain to friends, they didn't understand. It didn't make sense to them. I had so much going for me. Why couldn't I just snap out of it, be positive, forget, let go, get out of myself?

My pal Al never clearly understood my condition, but he never took it personally either. It was nice to have a long history with someone.

After a brief visit, I left his house and walked the few remaining blocks to the energy healer's three-story walk-up. I liked its location, across the street from the Hotel Lincoln where Lenny Bruce once worked the switchboard. I climbed the narrow, dark stairwell. I liked the old smell of the place, the layers of paint on the worn, warped walls, the sense of lost time, the residual energy of long-ago lives.

Her space was as bright as I remembered—the ceilings high, the fixtures ancient. New landscape paintings covered the walls. We sat and talked a while before I laid down for a healing.

She asked me when I'd had the pain last.

I told her I'd been up all night with it.

She asked if I could bring the pain up into my stomach now.

I thought, *How can I recreate the pain? It comes involuntarily.*

I said, "I don't think so, but I'll try to viscerally remember...."

Before those words were out of my mouth, the pain came billowing up from my solar plexus so fast and hard, I couldn't breathe. Tears squeezed out the sides of my eyes.

Instantly, I knew what it was. I said, "Oh, my God, it's sadness. It's old sadness."

She said, "I want you to try to picture your solar-plexus chakra."

I didn't know how I'd do that. I'd never pictured a chakra. I knew where they were, had a general idea what they represented and what colors each was associated with, but that was it.

Still, I gave it a try.

With my eyes closed, I silently asked my body/mind if I could see my third chakra.

I saw a flat opening about six inches above my stomach. It was very faint.

Ann asked, "What color is it?"

I looked and saw that it was gray, a sad, rainy day gray.

I said, "Gray."

She asked, "Is that the only color?"

"Yes."

And then, to my utter amazement, I saw a brown, rusted metal rod sticking up from the center of the chakra. It stood vertically about three-feet and was about two-and-a-half inches wide.

I panicked. I cried out, "I see a rod. A big, tall rod sticking out of my chakra. I want it out! I want it out! How do I get it out?"

Ann was very calm. She said, "Look to see if there is any other color there."

For a millisecond, I saw a splash of purple rise up the right side of the rod.

"Purple", I said.

She said, "Pour the purple into the chakra. Use whatever means you can imagine to do this. Pour the color in."

I imagined buckets of purple light pouring into the chakra. The rod lifted up as I did this, but it remained hanging there suspended.

Panic rose up inside. I called out to the spirit of my deceased father in my head.

I said, "Dad, Dad, please take this rod away. Please get it out of here."

Instantly, I saw his arm swoop in from my left and grab the rod. I watched, flabbergasted, as he walked away and out of my line of sight.

All of this occurred in a matter of seconds.

I immediately, intuitively, understood the rod was created when I was little to keep me from feeling unmanageable emotional pain—pain in response to what was occurring around me and the pain I'd already accumulated too much of inside.

I called out, "Goodbye, little rod, thank you for keeping me from feeling pain when I was little."

Ann said, "The rod is going to rod heaven now."

I burst out laughing. "Yes, little rod, go into the light, into rod heaven. Be transformed. Thank you again."

Since that moment, I've never again had that pain in my solar plexus.

Epilogue

All the pain I never felt sat waiting for me forty years.

Three years into releasing trauma and emotional energy, I no longer have the pain in my feet, legs, glutes, lower back, stomach, or neck, the pain in my face or head is less frequent, and I've discovered effective methods to calm my body down or pull myself out of despair, numbness or gross fatigue. I believe every new method with which I tried to heal my PTSD helped, with the exception of craniosacral therapy (due to a mismatch in therapists.)

One of the things I am most grateful for is the realization, at a visceral as well as intellectual level, that the hyperarousal and rage I used to find myself tripping into almost every day for a while was never due to something in my environment, but was simply my thinking brain trying to make sense of my internal state of emergency, grabbing at straws to explain it in order to give me an opportunity to release overwhelming energy. It was incredibly exhausting to live as if my wellbeing was completely dependent on other people behaving in some impeccable way.

My hypervigilance is still alive and well, but it doesn't keep me up like it used to.

Unless, of course, there is an emergency.

When I flew to Arizona to help my uncle, one crisis followed another and I did not sleep for the five nights I was there. I nearly collapsed in the airport on my way back home and it took me a month to recover, not just physically, but emotionally and spiritually, too. I cried several times a day for a while because of the anguish and sorrow I felt at seeing my dear uncle in such pain and discomfort.

But before I left, he did agree to in-house caretakers, so the visit was a success. He was safe and he didn't have to leave his home.

Two months later, my brother had open-heart surgery. I stayed by his side that first night in ICU and didn't sleep a wink. I stood by helpless when he flat-lined at one point as the doctors and nurses circled round and brought him back. Every day my brother was in the hospital, I'd visit as cheerful as could be. Then I'd go home and cry my little eyes out. I'm happy to report my brother healed beautifully.

A month after that, Jack had his aortic heart valve replaced. I'm happy to report he, too, is well on the mend. You can imagine my hypervigilance level was pretty high in the weeks before and after his surgery. The amazing thing is—when I did fall sleep, I slept well.

I find I recover faster from these crises and mini burn-outs if I set aside time daily for TRE, mindful meditation and/or a good cry. (FYI, I no longer feel sadness every day like I did for two years. Dare I hope I finally filled the bowl in my dream with my tears? Time will tell.)

There is no question I've released a lot of buried trauma energy and emotion in the last three years and it's made a difference in my quality of life and sense of wellbeing, but I have a ways to go.

I dream of a day when all that energy has been discharged and I feel so relaxed and safe at my core that when I go to bed at night, I fall deeply and quickly asleep. I remain asleep for a solid eight hours and wake in the morning rested, refreshed, and restored, excited to take on a new day free of hyperarousal, hypervigilance, fatigue, sadness and intrusive thoughts.

Someday, my poor overworked survival brain will no longer detect any signs of danger within or without. It will sit back then, relax and go on vacation.

I will be only too happy to do the same.

December, 2015

Postscript

By the way, before I left for Arizona, I took the driver's test, passed and got my license for the first time in forty years. If my sixteen-year-old self did, indeed, return to my soul, she must have been pleased. How she loved to drive! But if I really want to make her happy, I'll need to find the means to purchase a 1973 white Oldsmobile Cutlass Supreme with an eight-track tape player featuring Derek and the Dominoes, and take to the open road.

Hmmm...

....uh...Dad...

...how about another miracle?

Recommended Reading
(In alphabetical order)

Anatomy of the Spirit—Caroline Myss, Ph.D
Best book on chakras I've read.

Believe and It Is True—Deborah K. Lloyd
Inspiring. The author gets post-polio syndrome in middle-age. She tries alternative methods of healing with Reiki and a shaman and has surprising results.

The Body Remembers—The Psychophysiology of Trauma and Trauma Treatment—Babette Rothschild
Fantastic and illuminating. Case studies of PTSD clients, written by the therapist author. I loved how she kept her patients safe as they released trauma.

Buddha's Brain—The Practical Neuroscience of Happiness, Love and Wisdom—Rich Hanson, Ph.D. with Richard Mendius, MD
How to stimulate, strengthen and rewire your brain for greater wellbeing.

Coping with Trauma-Related Dissociation—Boon, Steele, Van der Hart
Revelatory. Includes workbook material. Very helpful.

The Courage to Heal: A Guide for Women Survivors of Child Sexual Abuse—Ellen Bass, Laura Davis
Although I am not an incest survivor, this book gave me one epiphany after another when I first read it in my thirties.

Dance of the Four Winds—Secrets of the Inca Medicine Wheel—Villoldo, Jendresen
All the books I list by Villoldo have to do with shamanism and healing. He frequently explains how the brain responds to trauma and the involuntary fragmentation of the self/soul in order to survive.

Denial—A Memoir—Jessica Stern
Riveting. How normal a dangerous life feels to the survivor of trauma! Our body/mind will recreate scenarios of potential trauma again and again in order to release the energy trapped in our nervous systems.

Energy Medicine—Donna Eden
The "bible" of energy medicine. Lots of techniques and simple healing exercises.

Energy Work: The Secrets of Healing and Spiritual Development—Robert Bruce
A good book about moving energy through your body to heal your body. Lots of exercises. The narrative isn't a laugh a minute, but the book is thorough and informative.

Focusing—Eugene T. Gendlin, Ph.D.
Incredibly powerful healing technique. To me, focusing is sort of a deep, focused mindful meditation of the body's felt-sense leading to all sorts of amazing experiences, including revelations and release of

pain. Warning: Body memories came up so quickly for me that I advise anyone with missing blocks of time to approach this method with caution. You may not remember, but your body does. You can always slow down or stop it if it gets too intense. Also, keep in mind some things might feel like body memories, but may instead be metaphors for what happened in lost time.

Eight Keys to Safe Trauma Recovery—Babette Rothschild
Good basic information.

Healing States—A Journey into the World of Spiritual Healing and Shamanism Alberto Villoldo, Ph.D.
Companion to the 12-part documentary. Visits with different kinds of healers and shamans in South America. Details experiences apprenticing to Peruvian shaman.

Healing the Folks Who Live Inside—Esly Regina Carvalho, Ph.D.
Explains EMDR (Eye Movement Desensitization and Reprocessing) Therapy.

Illumination—The Shaman Way of Healing—Alberto Villoldo, Ph.D.
He sees crises as initiations giving us the opportunity to become illuminated or awakened to our divine nature. Includes shamanic healing techniques and related discoveries in neurobiology. Talks about trauma and the brain.

Invisible Heroes—Survivors of Trauma and How They Heal—Belleruth Naparstek
A must-read. So inspiring. So illuminating. Simply wonderful.

In an Unspoken Voice—How the Body Releases Trauma and Restores Goodness Peter A. Levine, Ph.D.
He wrote this after his classic *Waking the Tiger* so it has updated and additional material. Great book.

Many Lives, Many Masters—Brian L. Weiss, MD
Fascinating account of skeptical Yale-educated psychiatrist stumbling upon the reality of reincarnation. A lot of healing stories, ideas and wisdom to contemplate as to the mystery of tragedy in human life.

The Power of Now—Eckhardt Tolle
Inspiring reading for living in the moment. Since the original trauma energy continually cycles through our bodies, it cannot be found in the past. Dealing with it in the now is the only way out. Gives helpful, easy-to-do techniques.

Shaman, Healer, Sage—Alberto Villoldo, Ph.D.
Well written book detailing techniques to heal the imprints of disease and trauma in our energy field. Fascinating true accounts.

Soul Retrieval—Mending the Fragmented Self—Sandra Ingerman
I read this cover-to-cover in one sitting. This is the book that first inspired me to meet with a shaman for soul retrieval.

The Tapping Solution—Nick Ortner
Excellent explanation and clear directions for this simple healing practice with many inspiring case studies.

Trauma and Recovery: The Aftermath of Violence—from Domestic Abuse to Political Terror—Judith Herman
A classic.

Waking the Tiger: Healing Trauma—Peter A. Levine, Ph.D.
If you read only one book on PTSD, I vote this be the one.

What Every Body Is Saying—An Ex-FBI Agent's Guide to Speed-Reading People—Joe Navarro
He interprets body language based on his knowledge of the survival brain and how it involuntarily controls body movement and positioning. Fascinating.

...

Best Novel I've Read about Childhood Abuse:
The Complete Patrick Melrose Novels—Edward St. Aubyn

Movies That Helped Me the Most in Regard to PTSD:
Life of Pi—After seeing this movie, I was able to forgive myself for things I previously couldn't.
Fearless—Great movie about dissociation. Explained to me why I was often so "fearless". (I was a courageous, little girl, but my fearlessness as a teenager and adult was often something else.)
Marnie—I first saw this in the sixties when I was a little girl. I was fascinated by the story and wanted to be just like Marnie—beautiful, impeccably appointed, completely independent, and emotionally inaccessible. Loved the score by Bernard Hermann. I don't know if Hitchcock meant to direct a movie so much about trauma as about a cool blonde, but it's all there—dissociation, flashbacks, numbness, despair, intrusive thoughts and so on.

Recommended PTSD Forum: MyPTSD.com
Although I am no longer a member of this site, I learned so very much from everyone when I was there. Take what you can use and leave the rest.

For Adult Children of Alcoholics:

Codependent No More—Melody Beattie

I never liked the self-help-sounding title of this book, but it is a must-read if you grew up with an alcoholic or live with one. It explains what happens to families with an alcoholic, how reality is denied, and how children take on one or more of four roles (caretaker, over-achiever, scapegoat and/or the one who acts out the family dysfunction) and go right on into adulthood in these roles, usually with unhappy results. I notice there is another book with the same title on Amazon, but it is a rip-off. The one written by Melody Beattie is the original.

About the Author

Ann E. Laurie was born on the South Shore of Chicago, grew up on the North Shore and, for the last forty years, has lived in downtown Chicago. She studied English Literature at the University of Chicago and worked in bookstores for many years before losing her soul to the corporate world and retiring. She lives in a cozy, high-rise cube with her husband, Jack, and their eight plants: Minty, Little Hearts, Beautiful, Basie, Ivy, Leprechaun, Little Momma, Westie and Lima Bean.

In 2016, she will publish a short memoir *Once There Were Bookstores in Chicago* as well as the trilogy *Woodlake Road,* a psychological thriller about good versus evil played out against the backdrop of the swinging sixties in Chicago's affluent North Shore. If you would like to be advised when this or any of Ann E. Laurie's new titles are released, please subscribe here: Ann E. Laurie New Releases.

If you have any interest in being a Beta Reader for future publications, please email yours truly at annelaurieauthor@gmail.com. I'd ask only for general feedback— what you liked and what you didn't. In return, I'd be forever grateful and, with your permission, thank you in the published book's Acknowledgements.

Dear Reader, I sure would appreciate it if you'd take a moment to review this book. It would be a great help to this unknown author, but please, under no circumstances, feel any obligation. Honestly, I'm just thrilled you read the book.

Thank you so much.

God bless you.

Other Titles by Ann E. Laurie

Summer in the City: 111th and Western
A nostalgic look back at the summer of 1969, when a visit with my grandmother—and one special book—brought light to a childhood gone dark.

Au Revoir, My Arthritis
How I got rid of the arthritis in my husband's feet, and what I did with the calcium deposits.

Startle: A True Story of PTSD and the Paranormal
When I was forty-nine, I began seeing apparitions in my apartment, which ultimately manifested in blacker-than-black figures. Was I hallucinating from sleep deprivation? Were they ghosts? Or were they darker energies? You decide. (This short-read is included in *PTSD: Frozen in Time* after this section, so please don't buy it!)

Ghostsmeller: Adventures of a Low-Status Medium
This short-read details the true paranormal adventures of a ghost-smelling medium and her understanding as to why, in middle age, she can suddenly interact with spirits. (This short-read is included in *PTSD: Frozen in Time* after this section, so please don't buy it!)

If You Enjoy the Writing of Ann E. Laurie, You'll Enjoy the Books of Lori A. O'Connell (See her guest essay following this section.)

Slouching Towards My Weltanschauung

Eighteen essays, most of which were written in jest, on subjects including Leni Riefenstahl, Simone Weil, Judge Judy, The Biggest Loser, mindful meditation, La Cosa Nostra, ghosts and ghost hunters, the author's painful feet, divine messages regarding vegetable packaging, burn-out, the top-twenty, bestselling intellectual books of all time (maybe), waking to pee through the night after age fifty, plants with PTSD, and a search for the magical Red Ball Jets.

Nicky Chase: Man in a Fish Oil Pill

The morning my husband and I found a tiny man trapped inside a fish-oil supplement, our quiet life of retirement ended and a strange, new world opened up—one where time proved not to be as linear as we thought, where teleportation and time travel were commonplace, and where history could be rewritten. Nicky Chase: Man in a Fish Oil Pill is a novel of human transformation and the triumph of the spirit.

My Husband's Toes

In February of 2012, my husband's toes began speaking to me. I came to know them intimately—their hopes and dreams, their thoughts and fears, and their conflicting desires of both transcending their structural limitations and accepting their lack of autonomy. I share these historic dialogues at the risk of great ridicule in the hopes that others will come forward and share what I know now to be true—our toes are alive, and they need to be heard.

To Wee or Not to Wee

Guest Essay by Lori A. O'Connell
Excerpt from Slouching Towards My Weltanschauung

This morning upon awakening, I briefly swore. I hate waking up because my bladder is full. It's bad enough getting up two or three times a night to pee, but just once couldn't I sleep in and wake slowly, luxuriously, without having to pee right away?

I stumbled to the bathroom muttering and relieved myself.

After I ascertained that Jack, my husband, was my Jack and not a clone, we embraced. Then I grabbed a tonic water and spilled my guts.

I said, "I haven't thought of any new inventions lately. It's bumming me out, man. I try to think about what inventions would make life easier. The only thing I can think of lately is a pee-remover. I hate waking up because I have to pee. If someone or something could remove the pee from me during the night so I could have a full night's rest instead of getting up several times, I would really appreciate it. Or it would be good if we could take a pill so we don't have to pee for weeks. Then one day a month, we could allot a couple hours just for peeing while getting a pedicure or reading a book."

Jack was stunned. "If only we had financing."

Then he went back to reading *A Pearl in the Storm* by Toni McClure. It's a really great book. She is this amazing person who decides to row alone across the Atlantic Ocean from the U.S. to France. No woman had ever done that.

She thinks it will take about three months. Things are kind of cool for a while. Alone on the sea at night with billions of stars above, dolphins come to visit and play. Enormous whales emerge just a few feet beside her. From time to time, a shark swims in circles around the boat for a few hours. She is so brainy and capable and fixes what gets broke in these tremendous storms. She's tough and strong and has no time for pain. She rows twelve, fourteen, sometimes seventeen hours a day. Then she gets caught in two or three hurricanes. She's smashed all over the place in her tiny boat. These fifty-foot waves are killers. The boat starts cracking up. Her bones are breaking when she's thrown from one side of the boat to the other. She doesn't know if she's going to make it. She loses consciousness at one point. I won't tell you the ending. You have to read it.

She weaves her life story into the narrative. At one point, while attending Harvard's Divinity School, she works in a hospital. She befriends a Jesuit who lies dying of cancer. As time goes by, she becomes overwhelmed by the tragedy she sees and comes into his room crying. He says to her, "You have to let your heart be broken by the things that break the heart of God."

I thought, *Now that is pretty good. I can live with that particular anthropomorphizing of God. This I can see as the only response God should have had to the Holocaust. His heart broke.*

I get upset with God when I read about the Holocaust. But then I have to remind myself that I am getting upset with an idea of God, not God Himself. How can I argue with an idea or have expectations or get disappointed by an idea of God someone thought up? But clearly the idea of a loving, interventionist God who looks out for the lilies of the field and has his eye on the sparrow did not exist at the time of Auschwitz. That's not to say that there is no God. I believe there is. But who God is—this I do not know.

From the books I've read by Karen Armstrong, it would appear that prior to the sixteenth or seventeenth centuries, people knew they couldn't get anywhere trying to rationally comprehend the incomprehensible reality of God. They valued ritual and myth and song and meditation and art as a bridge to God and used these means to transcend their humanity and experience the sacred.

Then people made all these scientific discoveries and were blinded by their own brilliance and decided that not only could human beings figure everything out, but that only true things were of value, things man could prove.

Yet the Bible was filled with myth and allegory and parable, and they weren't literally true. Was the Bible then of no value? Could the scientists explain God? They couldn't, but yet they wouldn't say, "I don't know." That lead to the idea that everything in the Bible literally happened. Genesis was real and all the rest. And if you doubted that, you needed faith and prayer and humility because God was great and you were dirt.

I do believe that people have one-on-one spiritual experiences. I just don't get why I don't get them. Or Primo Levi. When the S.S. guard said to a starving, beaten Auschwitz inmate standing in the bitter cold for hours without shoes, dressed in rags, forced to watch the hanging of prisoners who tried to escape, "Where is your God now?", it would have been the perfect time for God to appear and say, "Here I am you (expletive)." Then God would have shot the Nazi and all the rest before spiriting away all the camp prisoners to heaven. That would have been so cool.

If this was such a world where God intervened at Auschwitz, where else would He intervene? When any injustice occurred, any wrong done, any pain felt, any problem presented itself? Would it be based solely on what I perceived needed fixing?

If God intervened when I wanted Him to, then everyone would love me. They'd have no choice, of course, but still.... And I would not have to pee two or three times a night and first thing in the morning. We would all do without the bladder completely.

But we have to live life on life's terms.

Gandhi said, "Be the change you want to see in the world."

Tomorrow I begin work on the pee-remover.

If you enjoyed this essay, please consider downloading Lori A. O'Connell's book of essays, most of which were written in jest: Slouching Towards My Weltanschauung

Note from Ann E. Laurie:

I published the following two short-reads about PTSD and the paranormal previously. Because I am including them in this book unrevised, some parts may sound repetitive after finishing *PTSD: Frozen in Time*. Please forgive. Since they have more to do with the paranormal than releasing buried energy, I did not include them in the book proper. I hope you enjoy.

Boo!

Startle

A True Story of PTSD and the Paranormal

Ann E. Laurie

Every man takes the limits of his own field of vision for the limits of the world.

—Arthur Schopenhauer

Preface

When I was forty-nine, I began seeing apparitions in my apartment, which ultimately manifested in blacker-than-black figures.

Was I hallucinating from sleep deprivation?

Were they ghosts?

Or were they darker energies?

You decide.

Startle

I chose to live alone after college, primarily due to symptoms of PTSD.

That which I found most disruptive was a near-constant state of hypervigilance and tension. I was too frequently triggered into emergency mode by quite ordinary events. I'd startle at the drop of a hat—at the sound of an unexpected voice or quick movement in my peripheral vision—and feel energy inappropriate to the context. Big energy, violent energy, energy for fighting, for defending my life or running for my life. It was very difficult to discharge. It undermined my sense of well-being and significantly interfered with sleep.

By living alone, I cut down the chances of being inadvertently triggered. I slept better, my health was better and I could make a living.

Though I associated stress with living with people, I enjoyed socializing. I was personable and socially adept. I never lacked for dates if I wanted them. There was always a lot to do where I lived in downtown Chicago. Mostly, I liked to go to the movies or The Pump Room at the old Ambassador East Hotel where a trio played and my date and I danced to songs I'd heard growing up and watching old movies—"Laura", "As Time Goes By", "Moon River".

But I never let anyone get too close.

I knew myself.

I had to live alone.

...

By day, I thrived in a high-pressure, deadline-driven job. My near-constant internal sense of emergency matched the atmosphere of the office, giving me a Twilight Zone sense of calm. There was consistency then between my inner and outer worlds.

When I came home late at night and turned the key in the lock, my quiet, dimly-lit, book-lined, high-rise apartment was my safe place. I'd kick off my high heels and tailored suit, slip into comfortable clothes, make myself something to eat and curl up with a good book on the sofa.

But even with my carefully constructed life—the haven of my apartment, the careful control I imposed on my social life in never letting anyone get too close—the aftereffects of childhood trauma relentlessly followed me through the years, yapping at my heels like The Hound of Heaven. I rarely felt truly rested. Not down deep. Not for long.

I might fall into a relaxed reverie for a couple hours at night after work, sitting in the quiet with a good book.

But then I'd hear the exhaust-brake of a truck or someone dropping a heavy object on the floor above, and I'd freeze—adrenalin flooding though me like a lit-match to gasoline. It would take a while for my heart rate to return to normal.

I tried medication over the years, both doctor-prescribed and self-prescribed. The former was never particularly effective. The latter worked for a while—until I developed the inevitable tolerance and quit.

I never found a therapist or psychiatrist that was of any help beyond offering a compassionate ear or intellectual enlightenment because—with PTSD—the talking cure does not work. At least, it never did for me. It was my survival brain that needed engaging. And the survival brain only understands sensory information, not speech or words. (I was later to learn of effective somatic therapies, which theoretically discharge trauma energy, but I did not know of these techniques until years after the experience I am about to relate.)

...

By the time I hit my forties, I was burning out.

It was understandable.

There had been too many years of too much adrenalin, too many years of physical, mental and emotional stress, too many years of lousy sleep, isolation, depression, smoking, and not eating right. And the five years I was addicted to painkillers didn't help anything.

In the spring of 2005, my health began seriously deteriorating. I was unaware that what I was going through would be any different than all the other times in my life when I didn't feel well. I had always pushed through discomfort before and figured I'd go on like that until the end.

I never slept well to begin with, but now it was almost non-existent. I'd go a couple days without any sleep, then sleep two hours, then go without any for another couple days, and so on.

I had migraines constantly, but with a new twist. Whereas before, I felt pain in the eye area and overwhelming nausea, now I also felt like my head was going to explode.

I got terrible burning sensations in my feet.

I had intense stomach pain unpredictably.

I had constant acid reflux.

Sometimes my tongue swelled, making me sound like Humphrey Bogart. He sounded cool like that. I did not.

In March, I got a cold and it didn't go away for ten weeks.

I went to a lot of doctors. They found nothing wrong with me besides exhaustion and being run-down.

I felt so tired. More tired than I ever remembered.

It became difficult to get myself to work in the mornings. I began going in later and later, sometimes not arriving until early afternoon. I'd been there a long time and had always done an excellent job, so the CEO didn't mind too much. In fact, he said if I needed to work from home sometimes that would be fine as long as deadlines were met.

My eyes grew sore from sleep deprivation making it uncomfortable to read, so I began to spend my nights watching TV. But unless I found an absolutely riveting movie or documentary, I'd grow increasingly agitated as the evening wore on. I discovered that if I turned out all the lights, muted the TV, turned on the captions and watched the screen while listening to music on my headphones, I would sometimes grow drowsy and sleep.

One night, I was watching a Jack Lemmon/Walter Matthau movie. In the commercial, I noticed movement in my peripheral vision. I turned to see animated images on the surface of a glass poster on the other side of the room, nowhere near the reflections of the TV. I could see faces of people talking there.

I got up from the couch and walked over to the frame.

There was no movement there now.

When I walked back to the couch, I noticed talking-faces in the carpet.

Clearly, I was so exhausted that either the images from the movie remained projected on my mind's eye after I looked away from the screen or I was slipping into a dream state while I was awake.

I knew if I could just get a few nights of deep, uninterrupted sleep, I'd be fine. Still, given my sensitivity to unexpected movement, this business of seeing things that were not there was an unwelcome development. I made sure to keep my eyes on the TV screen or turn on all the lights.

I'd avoid looking at the floor.

A couple weeks later, as I sat in the dark watching TV and

listening to music, I saw in my peripheral vision three full-size, vaguely human-shaped forms moving towards me.

Startled, I turned quickly to look at them. They were not solid. They looked like pointillist images—shapes made up of tiny, translucent dots. Adrenalin shot through me like liquid fire.

I turned on the lights.

Nothing was there.

I never for a moment thought I was seeing ghosts or ethereal beings because I didn't believe such things existed.

I'd had great faith in God when I was a child and still believed, but in a more theoretical sense because in all the years I prayed and talked to him, I never felt his presence. God had become unreal to me, and yet I could never let go of the idea that he existed and heard me and would someday come through when I needed him most—in spite of his egregious absence through horrific events in the history of man's inhumanity to man.

But even though I was absolutely certain there were no supernatural or paranormal entities in the apartment with me, seeing these moving images was disconcerting. I could not control what my survival brain perceived as threatening. I was already having enough trouble sleeping. Now, I was really screwed.

I decided to always keep the lights on until I went to bed because I never saw anything when the apartment was brightly lit.

. . .

One night, as usual, I couldn't sleep.

It was about two in the morning and I was watching a documentary on political torture. I know it was not the best choice for someone in the shape I was in. I should have been watching something like *A Miracle on 34th Street*, but sleep deprivation seemed to reduce my I.Q. by half so that I'd find myself in a kind of trance-like daze watching all kinds of TV I would never have been interested in normally.

The documentary showed photos taken by military personnel of their prisoners in horrifying and humiliating positions. When I saw this, I leaped up from the couch and was so angry, I thought I'd explode. I started yelling—yelling at God for not intervening with those prisoners, for not intervening at Auschwitz, for not intervening in the death of a loved one the year before. I was swearing at God and throwing things. I'd never done that before, but clearly I was at a breaking point.

My frenzy did not last long. Maybe five minutes.

I felt completely drained then, and quickly prepared for bed.

I will never forget what happened once I got under the covers and turned out the light.

My entire bedroom was filled with beautiful orbs in all the colors of the rainbow. They were the size of softballs and indescribably beautiful—suspended in air, vibrating light. I thought God had sent me the equivalent of a Hallmark card. I was so happy. At last—after all these years—God had answered me.

I lay with my arms behind my head for a while staring with wonder at these translucent globes. Every so often, I'd reach out to touch one, but they were insubstantial. Much too soon, my eyes closed and I slept.

The next night, for the first time, I was eager to turn out the light at bedtime and see more orbs, or perhaps something even better.

But when I turned the switch, there was only darkness.

I lay on my side, facing the night table, and saw flickering images on the rounded body of the lamp there. I got up on my elbow and leaned in close. It looked like home movies were being projected on the surface. Tiny black-and-white home movies. It was hard to see with clarity who these people were. They were outside an old, white, two-story, wood-frame house somewhere, sitting at a picnic table, getting up and going into the house, moving in shaky, jagged motion, coming back out with supplies, enjoying some kind of get-together and smiling at the camera. I got the impression they were generations of an extended family. The era seemed to be the late 1940's or early 1950's.

Again, I was aware I was dreaming while awake. I found it interesting and distracting to watch my dreams while conscious. It also provided the added convenience of watching movies without having to get out of bed and turn on the TV. All that was missing were captions.

One night, at about three a.m., I turned off my bedside lamp and lay propped up on two pillows, one arm behind my head, waiting for my eyes to adjust to the darkness. Through the French glass doors of my bedroom, I could see the long, rectangular squares of city light pouring in through the floor-to-ceiling windows of the living room. My bedroom had no such brightness because I had placed a huge Oriental screen against the windows to block out any light that might interfere with my sleep.

I felt lazy and relaxed and hopeful I'd soon slip into easy slumber.

Suddenly, a blacker-than-black figure emerged from the Oriental screen. It was a man about six-foot tall. He moved quickly, with a purpose, toward the other side of the room. He emanated an evil so palpable that it raised the hairs on the back of my neck and along my arms. I instantly sat up, heart pounding, and turned on the light.

No one was there.

I was terrified.

Absolutely terrified.

Thus far, all the images I'd seen were hazy, innocent, neutral or dreamlike. This was something else. This figure was clearly defined. It had the vibrancy and tangible energy of a living thing. It was not dreamlike in any way. It felt real.

But how could that be? There were no such things as ghosts or demons. I had to have been having the equivalent of a night terror.

I went into the living room, turned on the lights, and smoked a cigarette.

A half-hour later, I tried sleeping again.

But not before going into my dresser drawer and digging out my grandmother's rosary and a small, white statue of the Blessed Virgin Mary, which I took to bed with me.

I slipped into bed, turned off the lamp and lay back.

As soon as my eyes adjusted to the dark, a black tarantula as big as my hand came scrambling towards me on the blanket at the speed of light. I leapt out of bed and turned on the lamp.

Nothing was there.

I stayed awake through the dawn.

The next night, I could not relax enough to sleep.

The following night, I was about to drop from exhaustion. I turned in at one in the morning. No blacker-than-black figure emerged nor did I see the tarantula. Instead, I saw about fifteen people in the living room. They weren't in living color, but in transparent shades of black and grey and dull white. They were in their thirties and forties, sophisticated and well-dressed. They seemed to be enjoying themselves at a cocktail party and paid no attention to me.

I was frozen for a moment watching them. I knew they didn't exist and if I turned on the light, they would disappear so I closed my eyes this time and kept them closed. Eventually, I slept.

Now, every night when I went to bed, I saw them there in the living room. I grew used to it. Though it was in a sense like watching the same film being played over and over, and I knew they were figments of my imagination, I couldn't help but experience them as intruders. It felt like my home was being invaded because my senses registered these visions as real and my body's chemistry responded in kind.

I began to throw up in the mornings from stress.

...

It was a great blow when I reached out to my family and they reacted with disbelief and hostility, accusing me of lying and taking drugs. My friends thought I was losing my mind and I felt them back off. My doctor told me I had a classic case of burn-out, which—in the old days—was called a nervous breakdown.

I was in a constant state of fight-or-flight now. But who was there to fight? Where could I run? I had no sense of safety—not at work, not at home, not walking down the street. Nowhere.

There were other terrifying manifestations. In the sliver of light at the top of the windows above the Oriental screen in my bedroom, I saw thousands of bugs swarming the surfaces. Particularly unnerving was a gigantic eye which appeared on my bedroom ceiling directly above my bed and looked down upon me each night unblinking. I hated having to squeeze my eyes shut and keep them shut when I turned out the light. It made me feel like a child. No amount of logic and self-talk could undermine the visceral terror of what I was living through.

The final assault to my sense of core stability and strength was the smell of human decomposition that came to pervade my space. I had to keep Vick's VapoRub dabbed under my nose in order not to gag.

I stopped going to work. I spent my days and nights sitting tightly crouched in the corner of the living room couch, feeling trapped, frozen, unable to move. I'd wait until my bladder felt like it would burst before walking to the bathroom. I paid the building's garage attendants twenty dollars to go to the convenient food store down the street to buy me cigarettes. When I could eat, I ordered in. I broke out in a sweat when I heard anyone in the hallway outside my apartment. I stopped listening to phone messages.

I had become like some pathetic character out of a 1950's B-movie.

...

Right before all this began, I had had dinner with a man named Jack. I met him quite by accident when I knocked on the wrong door in an apartment building and he answered. We had only gone out once before my nightmare began.

He told me later that he got a bad feeling that something was seriously wrong when I didn't return his phone calls and wasn't showing up for work. One day, the idea came to him to bring me groceries. When I heard his knock, I started shaking before walking slowly to the door. He identified himself and said he had groceries for me. I thanked him and told him I wasn't feeling well and to just leave them there outside the door.

He did this a few more times because he couldn't shake the overwhelming sense that something was fundamentally wrong. I never opened the door to him and strongly discouraged him from continuing to come by.

But then came the day I got my period and did not have the necessary supplies. No one answered in the garage. The only person I could think to phone was Jack. I knew he would probably be home because he was retired. I hated doing it, but I called and asked if he would go and get what I needed. I told him not to knock. (I couldn't bear the unexpected sound.) I would leave the door unlocked.

When Jack stepped into my apartment, he saw me sitting in the dark, curled up like a trapped animal in the corner of the couch. My once-beautiful apartment was filthy, every surface covered, the kitchen sink filled with dirty dishes, garbage bins overflowing, a layer of dust over all. He didn't say a word. He walked slowly over, laid the bag down on the table before me, and went into the kitchen where he quietly began to clean.

I sat on the sofa watching him like a hawk. Then, for the first time in a long time, I began to relax just a bit. His energy was calm and good and steady. He clearly perceived I was in a state of affliction and instinctively knew how to handle it.

When he finished the kitchen, he came into the living room and sat down across from me. I told him everything that had happened.

When I was done, I cried and cried and cried.

Then he said, "I don't care what you say, but I am not going to leave you alone tonight. I will stay on the couch, that's no problem. But I will not leave you alone."

I cannot express the feeling of relief and gratitude I felt. At last, someone didn't deny my reality, dismiss it, or back off. Someone was going to help me.

That night, when Jack was in the bathroom and I lay in bed, I looked up at the ceiling and the giant eye staring down at me. I smiled, turned my head to the bathroom and pointed, looked back up at the eye, and gave it the finger.

Slowly, it disappeared.

...

Jack stayed with me every night for the next few months. I quit my job and began sleeping again—long hours of deep, restorative sleep. The smell of rotting flesh dissipated. I no longer saw the cocktail party in my living room or the bugs or home movies on my lamp or the blacker-than-black figure or tarantula or the eye in the ceiling.

One day, the following spring, I woke and saw a man and woman near the Oriental screen in my bedroom. They were dancing in each other's arms the old-fashioned way, clearly in love. It was a beautiful vision and vanished too quickly. I got out of bed and went into the living room. The windows were open and the smell of flowers and freshly-watered earth filled the room. The leaves on the trees below glinted and flashed in the morning light. I felt healthy, happy and whole.

...

There is certainly a case to be made that I hallucinated the entire experience due to sleep deprivation. I think it would be within reason to attribute the animated images on the framed poster and the floor to fatigue and its effect on vision. Possibly also the "home movies" and even the swarming bugs.

A residual haunting could explain the cocktail party playing over and over—like the clip of a film endlessly repeating.

I believe it is possible darker energies were at work at some point, especially given the stench of human decomposition and the stark reality one can only know from first-person experience of a blacker-than-black figure emanating evil. The eye in the ceiling seemed to have an intelligence also, since it disappeared when I let it know it would no longer hold sway now that Jack was by my side. If that was the case, I believe the dark side knew the strength his support would give me. He was a good man of unshakable faith, and it didn't hurt—metaphorically speaking—that he was a retired fire fighter.

Sometimes dark energies see an opening when people are at their lowest. Perhaps the night I yelled at God with rage, disgust and despair, I unknowingly issued an invitation.

I do not think it was God who sent me the rainbow orbs, although anything is possible. It could have been from sleep deprivation or they may have been issued from a darker source—with a sick sense of humor as to what was to come.

I have since come to have great faith in God. I do not necessarily see him in the interventionist role I was given to believe in my youth. If man chooses to destroy others through murder or abuse or war, he does so of his own free will. If God interfered with that and intervened before any evil or unjust act could be committed, we would all live lives as puppets in a drama manipulated from on high.

Whereas I once displayed contempt in regard to supernatural and paranormal phenomena, I now have an open mind—not from virtue—but from the experience of having so many of my intellectual certitudes ripped asunder.

Life is a great mystery.

Sometimes it is terrifying, heartbreaking and incomprehensible. Sometimes it is beautiful beyond words.

Two years after my ordeal was over, I woke one morning with the ability to see auras around people. I began having pre-cognitive dreams and communicating with ghosts not ready to crossover. I have seen sparkling orbs and smelled heavenly flowers without source in our apartment nearly every day.

And when I say "our apartment", I refer to Jack's and mine.

Reader, I married him.

Ghost Smeller

Adventures of a Low-Status Medium

Ann E. Laurie

Dedicated to Annie Lyman, Dominic McGreal and Jim O'Connell,
the grandparents I never got to meet.

Reality is merely an illusion, albeit a very persistent one.
—Albert Einstein

I smell ghosts.

I've seen them. I've communicated with them. I've felt their palpable presence many times, but primarily—I smell them (also known as clairalience). So I kind of feel like I'm at the bottom of the barrel when it comes to being a medium.

My husband said there's nothing wrong with starting at the bottom and working your way up. Of course, I have no idea if I'll ever get a promotion. I don't know who's in charge. It's fine with me if I don't, though. In fact, I'd prefer not to because I have PTSD and startle often enough as it is. I don't need ethereal entities popping up all over the place, sending my blood pressure soaring and triggering me into greater states of hypervigilance and hyperarousal.

Still, despite my limitations, I've had some interesting adventures, a few of which I've gathered here along with my understanding as to why, in middle-age, I can suddenly interact with the spirit world.

...

For decades, I did not believe in ghosts. If I did smell, feel, hear or catch a glimpse of one, I chalked it up to something else. I never gave strange phenomena any significant thought or had any interest in the paranormal.

Much of my life was focused on ridding myself of PTSD symptoms, which were the result of childhood trauma. Particularly disruptive were the unpredictable bouts of hyperarousal, hypervigilance and explosive tension alternating with periods of dissociation in which I felt half dead—exhausted, numb and in despair at my inability to feel.

When I was forty-nine, I began seeing apparitions in my apartment. I was terrified because if there were no such things as ghosts and if I wasn't losing my mind, then what was happening? Need I say, being terrorized by dark entities exacerbated my PTSD.

But there was a happy ending. That was when I grew close to the man who would become my husband. Jack swooped in, shored up my waning strength, and stayed by my side until eventually the scene cleared.

I moved out and married Mr. Wonderful.

In the first few months in our downtown Chicago high-rise apartment, I did not experience anything paranormal nor did I expect to ever again. I thought that the infestation of energies in my old place was a one-time phenomenon.

Then one day, I was overcome with the most excruciating physical pain I had ever known. It felt as if someone were taking a sharp letter-opener and ramming it through my right eardrum over and over and over, day after day after day. No doctor could diagnose or fix the problem. If it had gone on any longer and I hadn't been married to Jack and I had had access to a gun, I don't know what I might have done. It was that bad.

Then one morning, about two months after the pain began, it stopped.

What bliss.

What quiet, gentle bliss.

But ever after, I had the most extraordinary sense of smell—and not necessarily in a good, super-hero way. Everything smelled way too strong. I was frequently sick to my stomach, even with smells I normally liked.

Strangely, the one smell that did not bother me at all was cigarette smoke.

Go figure.

Not long after, my father died. We had loved each other very much, but our relationship had been complex and fraught with misunderstandings and things left unsaid, though we tried to bridge the gap many times.

In the weeks following his funeral, I began having mystifying experiences.

When I laid down to take a nap in the afternoon and drifted off to sleep, I felt the weight of a two-hundred pound man sit down on the bed. Immediately, I'd jerk awake, irritated (sleep was hard to come by), and turn my head expecting to see Jack.

But no one would be there.

Still, it was obvious I was not alone.

Annoyed, I'd say, "Hey, you there! I'm trying to take a nap."

The weight would lift off, but by then I was triggered. With heart racing, all chance of sleep flew out the window. This continued happening for a couple weeks before stopping completely.

One afternoon, I was writing on the computer in our library. Jack was in the living room watching a documentary. Suddenly, I smelled paper burning. It was so pungent, I leaped from the couch and ran out into the hallway towards what I assumed would be the source of a smoldering fire. But the further I moved from where I had been sitting, the more the smell faded.

I backtracked to the couch. The smell was clearly localized there, as strong as ever.

I checked the outlets and all plugs.

Nothing.

I opened the window and took a whiff.

Nothing.

I stood on a chair and leaned into the vents.

Nothing.

The smell of burning paper permeated only that area where I had been sitting. I called Jack into the room. He smelled it, too. On impulse, I grabbed my new camera and took a photo. There, above the couch, hovered a perfect, white orb with a rainbow periphery.

Jack and I were stunned. We had never experienced such a thing.

But since there was nothing to be done, eventually he returned to the living room and I to my work in the library. The smell quickly dissipated.

I was back working for about half an hour when there came three loud knocks on the closet door a few feet to my left.

I whiplash-turned my head and stared at the door.

Clearly, someone was there. I could sense them.

In retrospect, I'm surprised I felt so little fear. I was more irritated than afraid because loud, unexpected sounds often triggered me into a state of hyperarousal, which could be time-consuming and difficult to bring down.

I said, "Please don't do that. If you are here in a supportive capacity, I appreciate it, but stop with the knocking. You're making my blood pressure go up and I need that like a hole in the head."

I waited a moment for a response. When none was forthcoming, I returned to the computer.

The next morning, I woke exhausted and bleary-eyed having had only a couple hours sleep. The apartment was empty. I saw a note from Jack that he was working-out downstairs. Pooped, I poured myself a Coke and took two Anacin with caffeine before flopping down on one of the dining room chairs next to the kitchen.

KNOCK. KNOCK. KNOCK.

I whipped my head towards the kitchen cabinets, my blood pressure skyrocketing.

I said, "Stop doing that! I don't feel good and you're making me nervous. You know I can't see you. Put yourself in my shoes. Geez."

Silence.

There were no more disturbances that day.

A week later, on Father's Day, I woke to find Jack in the kitchen just as he was about to leave to meet his daughter for brunch. He gave me a hug, saying, "Good morning, Angel."

For a moment, I was overcome with sadness that my father had never seen me in such a benevolent light.

I thought, *I wish my dad had thought of me as an angel.*

After Jack left, I sat reading the paper on the living room couch. There was no TV or radio or stereo on because I could never concentrate with background noise when I read. At one point, I stepped into the bathroom to freshen up. When I walked back into the living room, the TV suddenly turned on—blasting music at full volume. The Vogues sang out,

"You are my special angel,

sent from paradise,

I know that you're an angel,

heaven is in your eyes...."

The song was "My Special Angel."

I stood frozen, tears filling my eyes. Then slowly, I walked to the couch and sank onto the cushions, speechless, staring at the TV on a music station I didn't even know existed.

My dad had heard me.

It was one of the most thrilling moments of my life.

...

My mind now opened up to possibilities I had never before considered.

I began watching some of the shows on cable about ghosts and mediums and the paranormal. I researched online. I read a lot of books on the spirit world and related New Age subjects. Michael Crichton's *Travels*, Judith Orloff's *Second Sight*, Gerald Brittle's *The Demonologist*, and several books on shamanism by Alberto Villoldo were among the most fascinating and mind-bending.

Still, I didn't think I would necessarily experience any more supernatural activity. I assumed the song sent from my father was a final message. I figured it was he who sat on my bed those afternoons I tried to nap and he who created the smell of burning paper to get my attention.

Initially, I attributed the three knocks to him also, but then I wasn't so sure. Why would he do it again when I asked him not to? I had come across the theory that three knocks were the sign of a darker energy, that it was considered a mocking of the Holy Trinity and the hour that Jesus died. In the end, I wasn't sure what to think, especially after having dealt with negative energies in my previous apartment.

...

Early one evening, I was again writing in the library. Jack was in the living room flying on his flight simulator.

Finished with my work, I got up to see if he felt like ordering in for dinner. I stepped out into the hallway between the library and the living room, and nearly gagged on the smell of vomit. It was localized, about chest-high to me, right outside the library door. When I stepped two feet back, I couldn't smell it. Two feet forward, I could.

I called out, "Oh my God, Jack, come here please. Smell this."

He came into the hallway, got a whiff and backed off. "What the hell is that?"

Again, we checked every possible source: carpet, vent, window, bathroom, the hallway outside our apartment. It became quickly apparent that it was a ghost who, furthermore, was all over me like a cheap suit, following me wherever I walked, leaning into my right shoulder.

And, boy, was he making me feel sad.

Incredibly sad.

I sensed he was a poor, lost soul and not something evil. I grabbed my camera and had Jack take a picture. The photo showed an orb, and in the reflection in the kitchen window behind me was an old man on a cane.

I did not hesitate to speak, my throat thick with emotion.

"Spirit, you cannot stay here. This isn't your apartment. You smell very bad and it's making us sick. You have to go. If you are not aware that you are dead, I am telling you right now, you are."

And though I felt like an idiot, I said the following for the first time in my life: "You must go into the light. You must leave here and go where there is peace and love. Don't be afraid. All is forgiven on The Other Side. You will be with people who love you. You will feel so much better. If it were me, I'd be out of here in a second. Look around for the light. Go towards the light."

I kept repeating this kind of thing while opening all the windows, not that it helped with the stink.

The stress of this ghost was overwhelming. I felt increasingly desperate, urgently desperate, so much so that I called out to my dad for help.

Then, although I had never prayed directly to Jesus in my entire life, only to "God the Father", I knew he was portrayed as "The Man" when it came to showing compassion for those in affliction as well as casting out demons, so I called on Jesus, too.

Still, the vomit energy leaned into me.

I had no sage to smudge or holy water to throw. I wasn't that advanced in my paranormal dealings. All we had was a little, green Christmas candle. I didn't know if that would help, but I lit it anyway. I had nothing to lose.

Suddenly—and believe me, I know how bizarre and comedic this sounds—I felt compelled to play "The Greatest Hits of John Denver". I couldn't tell you the last time I played that album. It had to have been years. I went digging through our dusty CD collection in the library closet with Mr. Vomit hanging on me.

With tears in my eyes, I kept saying, "Go, go. Please go. Go into the light."

Finally, I found the CD and put it on the stereo in the living room, turning the volume on high. Jack and I sat on the couch with Mr. Vomit in my lap.

John Denver's voice sang out,

"There's a storm across the valley,

clouds are rolling in,

the afternoon lies heavy on your shoulders...."

Jack and I were singing along at the top of our lungs. Tears were rolling down my face. I thought, *Man, this is crazy.*

"...Hey it's good to be back home again...."

We sang along to every song on that album, holding hands and not moving an inch. Slowly, Mr. Vomit backed away. When the CD was over, he was gone.

I often wondered if my dad came for him, or Jesus.

Or if the ghost somehow told my soul he needed to hear those songs before he could leave.

Of course, it could also be he couldn't stand John Denver and I intuitively knew it would drive him away, especially with us singing along, loud and strong.

I don't know.

That's the drag of being a low-status medium. My abilities are so limited.

...

You can bet I went out and bought a bunch of sage sticks quick as a wink after that night. I was surprised to find I loved the smell of it and began smudging our place at least twice a week just for the aroma. Also, when I felt sick from strong smells, whether ethereal or material, it got rid of my nausea.

I began smelling spirits in our apartment several times a week, sometimes every day. I knew they were ghostly in origin because they were absurdly localized and without environmental source, and also because I'd always take a photo and see a corresponding orb. Jack smelled them half the time. He was more likely to see a shimmering in his peripheral vision and get shivers up his spine.

Some of the smells were beautiful. After Jack's oldest daughter unexpectedly died, I'd wake in the morning, walk into the dining room where Jack was having coffee and practically faint from the smell of roses. This occurred almost daily for a couple months. Last year, another of Jack's daughter's died and again, immediately after her passing, we would smell the most indescribably beautiful floral scent. It was what we imagined a flower in heaven would smell like.

My grandmother's delicious fragrance visited me often, especially when I was writing in the library. It seemed I was more accessible to Other Side energy when I was lost in creative pursuits, relaxed, meditating or in hypnagogic or hypnopompic states (between wakefulness and sleeping or sleeping and wakefulness.)

I have only smelled my mother a few times. Maybe she doesn't wear Chanel No. 5 much anymore.

I smelled my dad almost every day for a while. Sometimes I would sit on the library couch late at night, feeling him beside me, and say all the things I tried to say when he was on this side of the veil. I knew he understood me now. I knew he could "see" me now.

For a few months, I was very depressed because of an estrangement I felt between someone I dearly loved and me. I desperately wanted to fix it, to make things right, like they used to be, or as I thought they once were, but nothing I did worked. Sitting in the library one afternoon, I spoke with the spirits of my parents, asking for help. After a while, I went out to the kitchen to get something to eat. When I walked back into the library, a rectangular card was sticking up out of the couch cushions. I sat down and pulled it out.

It read, "No further action can be taken at this time without damaging the fabric."

I was blown away.

I could see it was a dry cleaning slip, but we had no clothes in the library. There was no chance whatsoever that dry cleaning bags had been laid down on that couch, and certainly not in the few minutes I was in the kitchen.

I had my answer. I knew what to do now. I would leave the situation alone. To force anything would have been a violence. It would all work out in time.

And it did.

...

Most of the time, though, I didn't recognize the identity of the ghosts or spirits. The variety of smells was mindboggling—horses, hairspray, beer, a delicatessen, newspapers, Windex, gasoline, newly-mown lawn, Johnson's Baby Oil, cheap shampoo, sweet grass, old-fashioned perfumed powder, tires, a stale cigar, men's hair cream, Palmolive soap, paint varnish, new leather shoes, firewood, pine trees, rubbing alcohol, lemons, Christmas candles, all kinds of perfumes and aftershaves...the list goes on.

I was never alarmed when the smells were pleasant. Most of my interactions went something like this:

"Hello, Spirit. You smell like Beemans Chewing Gum. What's going on?"

Silence.

Then I'd take a picture to see what kind and color of orb they were. I'd say a prayer for them to go into the light if they hadn't gone already. They rarely stayed more than a few minutes.

I couldn't understand why so many were passing through. At first, I thought maybe they were attached to some of the used-books I bought. Then I thought maybe they were floating around the building complex we lived in, which had over a thousand apartments. No doubt there had been quite a few deaths over the years. I'm sure, too, in the fifty years since the complex was built, there had been tenants who used Ouija boards. We also lived a block from one of Chicago's biggest hospitals, which, of course, housed a morgue. Our building was located only a couple blocks from both Lake Michigan and the Chicago River. Bodies of water are supposed to attract otherworldly energies as well as function as junctions between the Lower and Upper Worlds.

In the 1870's, the area beneath our building was part of Lake Michigan. When the City decided to build Lake Shore Drive, they dumped landfill here and created what became our neighborhood. The landfill was said to include the refuse from the Great Chicago Fire. Imagine the residual trauma energy from that alone.

Because so many of the spirits seemed to originate in the hallway leading into the library, I began thinking maybe there was some kind of opening there, a portal or vortex. When I'd stay up late reading, I'd often see figures peeking in at me from around that corner. They emanated a shy, friendly vibe, but still—it was disconcerting because it was always so difficult for me to relax and fall asleep.

Usually, I'd ignore them, but sometimes I'd say, "Hey! Cut that out. I'm trying to relax in here and you're raising my blood pressure!"

I'd get the sense that that would make them laugh, like it was a little game they liked to play.

I'd generally sense neutral, benevolent or innocent energies. When I'd nap on the library couch, I'd sometimes wake because of a tiny, childlike spirit gently tugging the pillow under my head. A few times, I'd open my eyes and see the shadow of someone leaning against the window ledge. I'd feel them just staring at me as if I were unaware they were there.

I'd say, "You know, I see you standing there. You think I don't see you? I see you plain as day."

They'd vanish then.

I'd also heard that, to the dead, mediums were like beacons of light in the darkness. Maybe when ghosts floated by our apartment, they saw light streaming out of my nostrils.

Seriously, though, I thought if these spirits wanted recognition, and somehow knew I could sense them, what was the point if that was about all I could do?

If I were a spirit wanting to communicate, I'd head straightaway to people like Theresa Caputo, The Long Island Medium or Kim Russo, The Happy Medium.

I didn't understand it. And I still couldn't figure out why, in middle age, I could suddenly connect with The Other Side.

...

Although the vomit-smelling ghost never returned, we had others that were just as unpleasant—urine, blood, dirty hair, flatulence, ammonia, foot odor, rotten eggs and more. But they almost always left immediately when I smudged.

Cleansing was a pleasant, calming ritual I practiced regularly whether I smelled ghosts or not.

I'd open all the windows and white-sage smudge the apartment from the right side all the way around counterclockwise. I'd say something to the effect of only spirits of love, light and healing were allowed in the space, all other energies were to leave and go into the light or go back where they came from. I'd say prayers for any visiting spirits or wandering souls. I'd ask St. Michael or Mother Mary to send angels to escort anyone needing assistance crossing over, and I'd ask God to bless our home. Every once in a while, I'd throw holy water in the corners of each room.

Then something strange began happening.

Every time I took the burning sage into the library hallway, the smoke alarm went off when it had never gone off before. Jack changed the battery, and still the alarm went off. This only happened when I passed through the doorjamb. As soon as I walked a few feet further, the alarm shut off.

One morning, about a month after this began, I was sitting in the living room. Jack had gone to take a shower in his bathroom, which was the "en suite" in the library. I heard him exclaim loudly and then come walking quickly into the living room, heading for the phone, saying, "I've got to call management. There's something wrong with the plumbing. You can smell the sewer in there. Check it out."

I walked into the library hallway and—oh-my-God—the smell of sulfur was so powerful, I could barely breathe. Still, I pushed forward into the bathroom and investigated all possible sources.

When nothing foul emanated from the sink, toilet, bath, faucets, vents, floor, or vanity, I knew it was a negative energy.

I stepped back into the hallway as it came pouring out, towering above me like a giant. I backed up, calling out to Jack to open the windows while I went for the sage.

When I smudged the living room, I saw a shaky, black X about two-feet high moving jaggedly through the air. I kept cleansing and saying prayers. By the time building maintenance arrived, it had gone.

After that day, the smoke alarm never again went off when I smudged the library, which suggests the negative entity had nested there for the weeks previous. I don't know why it broke out all of a sudden. Maybe it couldn't stand hearing Louie Prima's version of "Pennies from Heaven" one more time, since Jack played it every morning on his bathroom stereo speaker when he showered. Evidence was mounting that certain songs cleared out ghosts when Jack and/or I sang along loudly and off-key.

A lot of people think a sulfur smell is always demonic, but I don't think that's necessarily true. I don't think I could have gotten rid of it so easily if it were truly from "down under".

...

One night in the kitchen, I smelled mildewed clothes for an instant. I was sure it was the dishrag, but when I gave it a whiff, it smelled like Tide and Bounce. I gave the air a few more sniffs, but the smell was gone.

This happened a few more times in the week that followed, but since the mildew moments were fleeting, I didn't give it much thought.

Then one night, it welled up big as life by the microwave. I suddenly felt very tired, like I was going to pass out right then and there.

I laid down on the couch in the library, closed my eyes, and immediately sank into a trance-like state. I saw a young man, early twenties, blond, attractive, very muscular, lying on a silver metal rolling-cart, the kind you see in hospitals. I saw a wall of large, metal drawers behind him. He sat up in a panic, terrified. He had no shirt on. A white sheet covered his lower half.

He said, "I'm not supposed to be here! They don't know where I am! What they are writing on the clipboards is wrong!"

I realized he was in a morgue and woke up.

I thought, *Oh no, the poor guy. That's who I'm smelling. He must have died suddenly, unexpectedly, and is freaking out.*

I asked Mother Mary to send an angel to come get him and then said a rosary. When I was done, I took a photo of the portal-hallway and saw a dark shadow and a big white light. I'd like to say definitively he went with the angel, but a few days later, in the morning, for just a millisecond, I smelled him again. I sure hope I'm wrong and he's gone. I think it would be torture to exist between worlds, but they say we have free will after we die just as we had in this life. If a person doesn't want to move on, he doesn't have to.

...

Though somatic therapy, somatic release, meditation, working-out, and Trauma Releasing Exercises (see Berceli Foundation and YouTube videos online for TRE information) were terrific methods to communicate a sense of safety to my survival brain, I was still unpredictably triggered into states of hypervigilance and hyperarousal. Sometimes physical pain triggered an internal alarm and my body responded by flooding me with adrenalin and other stress hormones. But without any real danger in my environment, my thinking brain would often burrow madly inward searching for the source of perceived threat and then fixate on past events as possible culprits.

One spring, when I was in tremendous pain in my lower back and dupa, I'd sit up late unable to sleep and find myself going over and over a moment decades before in which I'd been unkind, castigating myself relentlessly, or I'd obsess over unjust acts, real or imagined, committed against me. This insanely compulsive and repetitive thinking seemed almost impossible to derail once it began and caused me great anguish.

One night a new foul-smelling ghost showed up. She smelled like perfumed poop.

I'd smudge and she'd go away, but then come back an hour or two later. This happened every night for weeks. She was never there during the day. She only came after Jack went to sleep and I was alone and lost in an obsessive mire of ruminating despair.

One night, I watched Kim Russo on *The Haunting of...*. She said some ghosts who regret how they lived their life will try to raise their frequency to get to a higher level on The Other Side by helping someone on this side who struggles with the same issues they did. Hours later, when I was once again alone with my pain and the tortured, hyper thoughts began churning, the perfumed-poop ghost returned. She smelled revolting.

I said, "Listen, I know you are there. I don't know why you won't leave. This isn't your apartment and I don't want you here because you smell bad. You should be cavorting on the Other Side in cascades of light. I don't know why you won't go, but you can't stay here. I can't see or hear you, so I don't know how I can help if it's help you need."

Then I thought, *What if this ghost is trying to help me?*

I said, "I suppose there is an outside chance you are trying to help me. Perhaps you have regrets about the way you lived your life. Maybe you see me doing something you used to do, something which undermined your wellbeing, and you are really sorry you wasted so much time doing that and you don't want to see me doing the same thing."

It suddenly occurred to me that I'd just taken a bubble bath and washed my hair and put on my favorite perfume in an effort to feel better, as I did every night, so I smelled really pretty—but my thoughts stunk.

Perfumed poop.

I said, "If, by any chance, you are trying to tell me to stop my obsessive, negative thinking, then I promise you I will. But the only way I'll know if that is why you are here is if you leave right now."

That's all I said.

I got up and walked slowly out of the room.

As I made my way, I sniffed and sniffed and sniffed.

Nothing.

No smell at all.

I retraced my steps, sniffing all the way.

Still nothing.

I walked thoughtfully to the door of the room and had my hand on the doorknob when all of a sudden the air around me was filled with the exquisite fragrance of Christmas candles.

I could not believe it.

The ghost had given me a gift.

After that night, when the old obsessive thoughts of regret or resentment began flickering to life, I'd think of that disgusting perfumed-poop smell and refocus my mind on something pleasant.

She never returned.

...

When medical tests ruled out organic cause for my pain, I knew it stemmed from buried emotional energy. The childhood trauma went on too long for the natural release of fight, flight or freeze energy.

When I was safe again, I was a teenager and began drinking, which stuffed the trauma energy down. After I quit in my twenties, I alternated between states of hyperarousal, hypervigilance, and dissociation. By the age of thirty, I was in tremendous physical pain. Every bone, muscle, joint, and tendon ached. My skin hurt, my head hurt, my eyes hurt. I had trouble breathing. I couldn't sleep and, eventually, I couldn't keep a job. Finally, a doctor gave me medication, which blanketed the pain and mercifully allowed me to sleep nightly for most of the twenty years that followed, but the meds also numbed my senses, my emotions and my body.

In my late-forties, these medications became less and less effective. I stopped taking them completely in my fifties. I realized then I had to feel and release the old emotional pain to heal or it would manifest in physical pain forever.

Anger was easier to deal with than sadness. I generally used the tremendous energy it gave me safely and productively by working-out—running, weights, aerobics, dancing, punching bags, whacking tennis balls.

Releasing sadness was another matter.

I cried easily enough with contemporary, real-time sad scenarios. The problem was releasing the ancient feelings of grief, loneliness, abandonment, betrayal, despair and anguish, which had been kept down forty years.

When I was somehow able to access that bed of feeling and cry, my physical pain went away.

For a while.

Until another round of emotional energy emerged.

If I could have, I would have cried like a baby for an hour every morning to live the rest of the day pain-free. But there came a point when I had exhausted the cathartic power of every heartbreaking song on my iPod and didn't know what else I could do to jumpstart the tears. Somatic therapists, energy healers, and shamans helped, but the old sadness ran deep.

One summer, I was in severe pain. I could barely walk. Sitting was torture. I could stand without too much pain if I leaned on one leg. I was only comfortable lying flat on my back.

Doctors and physical therapists at rehab centers could not help me, but I found a chiropractor who did. Progress was slow, though. I'd try to avoid allowing the pain to dominate my life by working on small projects around the house. One afternoon, as I folded laundry, I picked up the energy of a spirit who smelled like an onion. It was too mild to be offensive, but politely insistent in a gentle way so that I finally said, "Hello, Onion Spirit. What's happening?"

I emptied my head of thought for a minute—my way of listening. Then it was as if my soul received a telegram.

You need to cry now.

I made the connection between peeling onions and tears and said, "Good one, Spirit! You're telling me I need to cry, right? If you are, I'm all for it, but you have to help because I can't do it on my own anymore. I try and try, but the tears won't come."

The onion spirit persisted.

I said, "Okay, I'll try, but you'll see. The well has gone dry."

I went into the bedroom and closed the door. The entire room smelled like Noxzema, a smell I once associated with healing.

I said, "Hello, Noxzema Spirit. I remember your smell from childhood."

I laid down on the bed, closed my eyes and said, "Help me."

I didn't try to think of anything specific. I just relaxed and felt the pain in my body without editorializing.

A few minutes later, the tears came.

The Onion and Noxzema Spirits visited a couple times a week through the summer. By September, my back and dupa pain was gone.

Sometimes I think those weren't ghosts or spirits at all.

Sometimes I think they were angels.

...

One day, I realized that I began seeing apparitions in my old apartment about the time the medications I'd been on all my life stopped working. And I began smelling, and to a lesser extent, seeing, feeling and communicating with ghosts about the time I stopped taking all medications completely.

When I heard a medium say that children who experience trauma were more likely to develop psychic ability, I finally understood why

I was sensing spirits for the first time in middle-age.

It was because I could feel again.

After decades of being numb, I could feel.

And my senses proved to be as keenly sharp in my late-forties and early fifties as they were when I was a child and my senses became so overdeveloped in order to survive.

Mindful meditation, which I'd begun practicing to create a greater sense of wellbeing, enhanced these abilities exponentially. I started seeing auras around people, having pre-cognitive dreams (never good news), and seeing ghosts and sparkling orbs with the naked eye. I had flashbacks to previous lives—late 1700's Padua, Italy where I was an engineering student (and a guy!) rooming with Jack, also a student. Our apartment was infested with demonic entities, but Jack wouldn't believe me. I also flashed-backed to Paris when the Nazis rolled in. (Shudder.)

When I began practicing Eugene Gendlin's Focusing (an intense mindfulness of the body's felt-sense), I was blown away by hallucinatory and epiphanic experiences. (I advise caution in approaching Focusing if you have lost blocks of trauma time. Body memories and lost memories can emerge quickly.)

I went through a period when I despaired of ever finding my way back "home" again—of feeling at ease and safe within my body, myself and the world. Much as I liked the idea of identifying my journey with that of Joseph Campbell's hero, I couldn't imagine how I'd ever return to a state of pre-trauma wholeness without some kind of map or signposts to show me I was on the right path. I often felt like I was feeling my way in the dark.

One afternoon, I laid down to meditate. Twenty minutes in, a bat spirit-animal flew up into my face so quickly, I broke out of the trance and snapped my eyes open. His message was clear. Bats fly at night by echolocating—emitting sounds and listening for return echoes to determine their location and guide them to their journey's end. The bat was telling me I did not need to see where I was going in order to get where I needed to go. I could use my senses. I could feel my way home.

I like to think that's why so many ghosts came to visit—they could see I was finding my way home in spite of the darkness and figured maybe I could help them find their way, too, on the wings of a prayer. And perhaps some of them, after going into the light, came back to give me a hand because they could see how slowly I moved— feeling my way in the dark.

Postscript

I still smell ghosts and spirits every day. I feel them more frequently now. Sometimes they feel like dense atmospheric energy and other times like clouds or velvet-air enveloping me in a benevolent or loving way—like they are giving me hugs. I like that when they are angels, family or the equivalent, but I don't always know. So I've begun a daily practice of visualizing light and boundaries around me because I don't like people getting in my personal space without permission. (Angels, family and friends are always welcome.)

At night, I create a sacred space of healing and rest in the bedroom before I lay me down to sleep because I don't like ghosts waking me up with smells or pressure on my chest or freezing air. I do this by calling upon the angels as well as the Spirits of the Four Directions, Mother Earth and Father Sky.

Lately, most of the ghosts I see are striding quickly and purposefully down our entry hall or library hall as if they are cutting through on their way to somewhere else. They don't pay us a bit of attention. Maybe our home is the equivalent of an alley between dimensions, some kind of shortcut.

Thankfully, I still don't hear ghosts speaking out loud. I suppose they could be, but I can't hear them because I am hard of hearing. They seem to talk loudly, and even yell, by the strength and pungency of their smells, which I can often interpret metaphorically. When they have spoken in words, it's been telepathically in dreams and deep trance states.

My abilities are becoming more refined, little by little, but I cannot say I've been promoted. I remain primarily a ghost smeller, a low-status medium.

And that's okay with me.

2014

www.ingramcontent.com/pod-product-compliance
Lightning Source LLC
Chambersburg PA
CBHW030442290526
45786CB00001B/411

* 9 7 8 1 5 2 3 4 0 4 6 5 0 *